Richard Dayringer, ThD
David Oler, PhD
Editors

D0080352

The Image of God
and the Psychology of Religion

The Image of God and the Psychology of Religion has been co-published simultaneously as *American Journal of Pastoral Counseling*, Volume 7, Number 2 2004.

Pre-publication
REVIEWS,
COMMENTARIES,
EVALUATIONS . . .

The Image of God
and the Psychology of Religion

The Image of God and the Psychology of Religion has been co-published simultaneously as *American Journal of Pastoral Counseling*, Volume 7, Number 2 2004.

The *American Journal of Pastoral Counseling*™ Monographic "Separates"

Below is a list of "separates," which in serials librarianship means a special issue simultaneously published as a special journal issue or double-issue *and* as a "separate" hardbound monograph. (This is a format which we also call a "DocuSerial.")

"Separates" are published because specialized libraries or professionals may wish to purchase a specific thematic issue by itself in a format which can be separately cataloged and shelved, as opposed to purchasing the journal on an on-going basis. Faculty members may also more easily consider a "separate" for classroom adoption.

"Separates" are carefully classified separately with the major book jobbers so that the journal tie-in can be noted on new book order slips to avoid duplicate purchasing.

You may wish to visit Haworth's website at . . .

http://www.HaworthPress.com

. . . to search our online catalog for complete tables of contents of these separates and related publications.

You may also call 1-800-HAWORTH (outside US/Canada: 607-722-5857), or Fax 1-800-895-0582 (outside US/Canada: 607-771-0012), or e-mail at:

docdelivery@haworthpress.com

The Image of God
and the Psychology
of Religion

Richard Dayringer, ThD
David Oler, PhD
Editors

The Image of God and the Psychology of Religion has been co-published simultaneously as *American Journal of Pastoral Counseling*, Volume 7, Number 2 2004.

The Haworth Pastoral Press®
An Imprint of The Haworth Press, Inc.

New York • London • Victoria (AU)
www.HaworthPress.com

Published by

The Haworth Pastoral Press, 10 Alice Street, Binghamton, NY 13904-1580 USA

The Haworth Pastoral Press is an imprint of The Haworth Press, Inc., 10 Alice Street, Binghamton, NY 13904-1580 USA.

The Image of God and the Psychology of Religion has been co-published simultaneously as *American Journal of Pastoral Counseling,*™ Volume 7, Number 2 2004.

Cover design by Kerry E. Mack

Library of Congress Cataloging-in-Publication Data

The image of God and the psychology of religion / Richard Dayringer, and David Oler, editors.
     p. cm.
     ". . . has been co-published simultaneously as American journal of pastoral counseling, Volume 7, number 2 2004."
     Includes bibliographical references and index.
     ISBN 0-7890-2760-7 (hard cover : alk. paper)–ISBN 0-7890-2761-5 (pbk : alk. paper)
     1. God. 2. Image of God. 3. Pastoral counseling I. Dayringer, Richard. II. Oler, David. III. American journal of pastoral counseling.
  BT103.I45 2005
  231–dc22   2004021407

Indexing, Abstracting & Website/Internet Coverage

This section provides you with a list of major indexing & abstracting services and other tools for bibliographic access. That is to say, each service began covering this periodical during the year noted in the right column. Most Websites which are listed below have indicated that they will either post, disseminate, compile, archive, cite or alert their own Website users with research-based content from this work. (This list is as current as the copyright date of this publication.)

(continued)

* **Exact start date to come.**

*Special Bibliographic Notes related to special journal issues
(separates) and indexing/abstracting:*

- indexing/abstracting services in this list will also cover material in any "separate" that is co-published simultaneously with Haworth's special thematic journal issue or DocuSerial. Indexing/abstracting usually covers material at the article/chapter level.
- monographic co-editions are intended for either non-subscribers or libraries which intend to purchase a second copy for their circulating collections.
- monographic co-editions are reported to all jobbers/wholesalers/approval plans. The source journal is listed as the "series" to assist the prevention of duplicate purchasing in the same manner utilized for books-in-series.
- to facilitate user/access services all indexing/abstracting services are encouraged to utilize the co-indexing entry note indicated at the bottom of the first page of each article/chapter/contribution.
- this is intended to assist a library user of any reference tool (whether print, electronic, online, or CD-ROM) to locate the monographic version if the library has purchased this version but not a subscription to the source journal.
- individual articles/chapters in any Haworth publication are also available through the Haworth Document Delivery Service (HDDS).

The Image of God
and the Psychology of Religion

CONTENTS

ABOUT THE EDITORS

Richard Dayringer, ThD, is Adjunct Professor in the Bioethics Center at the Oklahoma University College of Medicine in Tulsa. He holds a Doctor of Theology degree from New Orleans Baptist Theological Seminary. Dr. Dayringer is certified as a Chaplain Supervisor by the Association for Clinical Pastoral Education and as an Approved Supervisor by the American Association for Marriage and Family Therapy, and is a Diplomate of the American Association of Pastoral Counselors. He is the author of five books, has published more than 70 articles in medical and theological journals, and is Editor of the *American Journal of Pastoral Counseling*. Dr. Dayringer served as a chaplain at Ground Zero in New York City for three weeks during October 2001.

David Oler, PhD, is Rabbi of Congregation Beth Or in Deerfield, Illinois, and President of the Association of Humanistic Rabbis. He earned a PhD in psychology at the University of Maryland and is a licensed clinical psychologist in Illinois and a Diplomate of the American Association of Pastoral Counselors. In addition to having a private practice providing psychotherapy and supervision, he has taught graduate courses in psychology on the adjunct faculties of Argosy University and in the Chicago School of Professional Psychology.

Foreword:
From Anthropopathism
to Transformational Religious Behavior

Anthropopathism, the projection onto the God image of human affective qualities, is much more at the heart of understanding human perception of God than is anthropomorphism, the projection onto God of human physical attributes. The latter is generally rationalized as metaphoric, scripture "speaking in the language of man," to help humans be able to conceptualize about God. Much more significant is the presentation of God as having human feelings, such as anger, jealousy, love, compassion, and regret. While some of these have caused considerable consternation and further rationalization and justification, ultimately any characterization of divine personality by projection of human affective qualities is a diminution of the divine by the human. The notion of a relationship with God is of necessity both anthropomorphic and anthropopathic.

Heschel's (1951) concept of having a sense of wonder and his related idea about radical amazement regarding that mental capacity is focused ultimately on human recognition of the awesomeness of the very mystery of God. However, numinous sensation tends to be particularized and, therefore, diminished by human projections. Emotional development involves

[Haworth co-indexing entry note]: "Foreword: From Anthropopathism to Transformational Religious Behavior." Oler, David. Co-published simultaneously in *American Journal of Pastoral Counseling* (The Haworth Pastoral Press, an imprint of The Haworth Press, Inc.) Vol. 7, No. 2, 2004, p. xv-xx; and: *The Image of God and the Psychology of Religion* (ed: Richard Dayringer, and David Oler) The Haworth Pastoral Press, an imprint of The Haworth Press, Inc., 2004, p. xi-xvi. Single or multiple copies of this article are available for a fee from The Haworth Document Delivery Service [1-800-HAWORTH, 9:00 a.m. - 5:00 p.m. (EST). E-mail address: docdelivery@haworthpress.com].

http://www.haworthpress.com/web/AJPC

becoming aware of subjective projections and moving beyond transferential stances. The same is true for spiritual development.

Wellhausen's (1894) documentary hypothesis concerning scriptures, explaining how differing names of God are at the core of distinguishing different segments of the Pentateuch, is a crystallization of earlier rabbinic teaching concerning the differing qualities or characteristics of God conveyed by the various names of God. Perhaps the various tribes or biblical authors had differing perceptions of God's affective qualities.

Religions tend to anthropopathically project onto God or other "divine human figures" ideal human qualities such as compassion. The adherents of these faiths are then encouraged to emulate those qualities. Such is the case with Jesus in Christianity, Buddha in Buddhism and with God in Judaism. An example from the Midrash:

> These are the ways of the Holy One: 'gracious and compassionate, patient, abounding in kindness and faithfulness, assuring love for a thousand generations, forgiving iniquity, transgression, and sin, and granting pardon. . .' (Exodus 34:6-7). This means that just as God is gracious and compassionate, you too must be gracious and compassionate. (Sifre Deuteronomy, Ekev)

We conceive of God in "our image," in idealized human terms, as the epitome of what we can possibly surmise God's qualities to be, and we are instructed then to imitate God.

Many religious teachings intending moral enhancement are based on human efforts to make sense of the mystery of God through a specific set of anthropopathisms and the related myths in which they are couched.

Process theology, like other more natural, rational, humanistic religious ideologies, is a great stride in evolving beyond the unexamined traditional religious practice of delimiting the concept of God by the projection that God is a "being." Seeing the "process" exclusively as a human endeavor, utilizing the high ideals one can conceptualize for the purpose of aspiring toward holiness, involves a deconstruction of anthropopathic projections. In this context holiness can be understood as moral aspiration, character development and human individuation. Any conceptualization of God's reality other than in such terms is, of necessity, of human making and is idolatrous in an ultimate sense.

Merle Jordan (1986) defined an idol as "anything that is raised to an absolute, the finite elevated to the level of the infinite or the transitory given the status of the permanent." The concept of operational theology refers to an individual's deepest feelings about God, as opposed to cognitive theology, which is really learning about someone else's operational theology that has often been articulated as a revelation. Thus, operational theology concerns an individual's personal idolatrous notions stemming from his or her anthropopathic projections.

Rizzutto (1979) proposed understanding the perceived image of God in the context of object relations theory. My doctoral dissertation (1999) researched perceived image of God from an affective perspective through the prism of attachment theory. One's object relations or attachment style is understood to reflect one's Weltanschauung, or worldview, and is, thus, related to one's perception of God. Both object relations theory and attachment theory focus on the relationship with one's primary caregiver in childhood as determinative of one's approach to or style in subsequent relationships. These relationships would logically include one's "operational theology," that is, one's relationship with or perception of God.

Attachment theory differentiates individuals on the basis of their approach to the seeking of personal security. The theory provides for four attachment styles, involving a positive or negative view of self and other and, thus, can be used to understand the different possible combinations of self and other perceptions that can also be utilized in understanding relationship with God. For example, the Preoccupied style of attachment involves a negative view of self and a positive view of other. This might lead to the seeking of external affirmation in relationships. From this perspective, one could understand prayer and other ritual observance as an effort to elicit acceptance and affirmation from God.

My dissertation utilizes Gorsuch's (1968) Wrathfulness scale, which is a measure of God's perceived affective qualities ranging from wrathful to kind. This appears to be akin to the qualities of justice and compassion conveyed by the divine names of Elohim and Adonai, respectively, in Hebrew scripture. One's style of attachment includes one's perception of the other's affective attitude toward oneself. The perception of God's attitude toward the self, whether it be wrathful or kind, is at the core of operational theology as anthropopathically derived.

Early psychoanalytic theorists addressed the concept of God in the context of their respective conceptualizations of the development of the human psyche. Freud (1910) understood God to be an illusion, an imago of one's father. While Jung (1913) differed from Freud in this regard, he did not commit to the reality of God as a living being. Jung (1936) suggested that the archetype of God is an inherited construct, the content of which develops individually in the human mind. Ultimately, Jung is positing a deeper source in the unconscious, the collective unconscious, for the construct God, and it is possible to interpret him as intending that its specific archetypal expression is the individual's anthropopathic projection of the perceived image of that construct.

Freud suggests that human development involves a transition toward a rational, i.e., non-theistic, perception of the world. Recognizing that religion helped shape human character and morality, he intimates that it would be better to be moral for intrinsic reasons rather than for fear of divine punishment, and construes religion as a representation of the super-ego. Both psychology and religion have a place in fostering the empowerment of the individual in terms of intrinsic character development without the intimidation of denigrating, infantilizing threats of punishment, including that of exclusion from ultimate redemption.

A theology of extrinsic salvation places authority over the individual's destiny with God, while a theology of intrinsic salvation empowers the individual to strive toward holiness without projecting the authority to judge his or her life onto an anthropopathic God. One way to conceptualize spiritual development would be as the movement toward an autonomous, self-actualized stance of intrinsic salvation theology devoid of anthropopathic projections of demanding, jealous, punitive, or rewarding qualities onto the God image. Both psychology and religion have the responsibility to provide the resources to enable such human spiritual evolution.

Such progress is stymied by chauvinistic and other deleterious attitudes fostered by various religious communities. An understanding of the origin of such notions may serve to deconstruct them. For example, the particularistic concept of being part of a chosen people is likely stimulated and sustained by sibling rivalry that emanates from the insecure Preoccupied attachment style perception of God, involving an anthropopathically projected conception of God's nature in making such a choice. This is a denigration of the concept of God, resulting from the emotional need for self-aggrandizement by various religious groups. Resolution of such needs has the potential to help foster a more universalistic, pluralistic outlook, for in the final analysis each human being faces the same ultimate mystery of God. Particularistic notions and the historical anthropopathisms of individual faith communities are stumbling blocks on the path to accepting the modest circumstance of the human being in the context of eternity and limited capacity to comprehend the mystery of existence. As the Talmud teaches (Avot IV: 4): "Be exceedingly humble, for a mortal's hope is but the grave."

From a psychotherapeutic perspective, traditional religious observances, including prayer, which often involves the adulation of God, such as through the frequent use of appellations such as "King," coupled with self-denigration, reinforce dependency, disempowerment, shame and anxiety about how one is "seen" by God. Enlightened religion, by definition, entails helping people transcend such notions. It is rare to experience traditional liturgies that express a yearning by the individual to be more kind and compassionate or more whole.

Ken Wilbur (1997) suggests that the most meaningful religious experiences are those that are transformational, i.e., leading to significant change in the spiritual and emotional functioning of the individual and of one's way of being in the world, as opposed to religious experiences that involve the seeking of comfort, affiliation and acceptance from others, including God. Transformation requires a giving up of external dependencies based on an honest recognition and acceptance of one's mortality and finiteness.

Religion and psychology have the responsibility to help shatter the complacency stemming from anthropopathic idolatrous notions that offer misguided comfort in the face of human fragility in the world. Religion and psychology can help people achieve detachment from religion's dependencies motivated by the search for security. Instead, a rational approach to religious resources and the serious pursuit of understanding through religious and psychological introspection can facilitate a new worldview freed of dependency on supernatural extrinsic salvation. The development of this capacity for emotional and religious independence is itself a transformational experience that can empower human beings to pursue holiness and progress toward intrinsic salvation.

David Oler, PhD

REFERENCES

Freud, S. (1910). Leonardo Da Vinci and a memory of his childhood. Vol. 11 in _____*The standard edition of the complete psychological works of Sigmund Freud*, vols. 1-14. London: Hogarth Press. 1953-1974.

Gorsuch, R.L. (1968). The conceptualization of God as seen in adjective ratings. *Journal for the Scientific Study of Religion, 7*, 56-64.

Heschel, A.J. (1951). *Man Is Not Alone*. New York: Farrar, Strauss and Young.

Jordan, M.R. (1986). *Taking on the Gods: The Task of the Pastoral Counselor.* Nashville: Abingdon Press.

Jung, C.G. (1913). *The theory of psychoanalysis.* In C.G. Jung, *Critique of Psychoanalysis.* Princeton, NJ: Princeton University Press, 1975.

Jung, C.G. (1936), The concept of the collective unconscious. In *Collected Works.* Vol. 9, Part I. Princeton: Princeton University Press, 1959.

Oler, I.D. (1999). *Attachment Styles, Parental Caregiving and Perceived Image of God. Doctoral dissertation, University of Maryland, U.M.I. Dissertation Services, AAT9942984.*

Rizutto, A.M. (1979). *The birth of the living God: A psychoanalytic study.* Chicago: University Press.

Wellhausen, J. (1894). *Israelitsche und Judische Geschichte.* Berlin: G. Reimer.

Wilber, K. (1997). A Spirituality that Transforms. *What is Enlightenment.* 12:22.

Preface

This collection is a thematic volume on the subject of the image of God. Of course, the popular image of God which most of us incorporated as children is that God is an old man with long white whiskers who lives in the sky and looks down on us with an all-seeing eye. The late great literary figure John Gardner wrote of God as an old man in the clouds–"bespectacled old Yahweh scratching his chin through his mountains of beard."

Another image of God that I have often heard from my counselees is that God is like "an oblong bluhr." Many have also revealed that God's voice is something like the voice of their fathers.

The image of God is a special interest of one of the members of the Editorial Board of the *American Journal of Pastoral Counseling*, Rabbi David Oler, PhD. His doctoral dissertation was on the image of God. He is also the person who solicited most of the manuscripts for this volume.

I think you will find this volume most interesting. It is heavy on empirical research which is perhaps somewhat unique for this subject. The authors are, with one exception, publishing in this collection for the first time. Please read on. You will be challenged and enlightened.

Richard Dayringer, ThD

[Haworth co-indexing entry note]: "Preface." Dayringer, Richard. Co-published simultaneously in *American Journal of Pastoral Counseling* (The Haworth Pastoral Press, an imprint of The Haworth Press, Inc.) Vol. 7, No. 2, 2004, p. xxi; and: *The Image of God and the Psychology of Religion* (ed: Richard Dayringer, and David Oler) The Haworth Pastoral Press, an imprint of The Haworth Press, Inc., 2004, p. xvii. Single or multiple copies of this article are available for a fee from The Haworth Document Delivery Service [1-800-HAWORTH, 9:00 a.m. - 5:00 p.m. (EST). E-mail address: docdelivery@haworthpress.com].

Liberating Images of God

Cynthia Stone, PhD, MDiv

SUMMARY. God images are constructed out of personal and cultural contexts. Expressing ultimate value and meaning, they are inevitably connected to self images. Pastoral counselors are uniquely qualified to relate to and assist in the transformation of these images. This paper discusses the constriction and impoverishment of God images due to traditional restriction of God images to those that are male and personified. Such traditional views are seen as part of a patriarchal, dualistic, literal mindset which has been challenged for several decades by a more holistic, fluid, pluralistic mindset, exemplified by quantum theory. The client and counselor's co-creation of more multiple and fluid images of God which embrace the feminine as well as the masculine, the nurturer as well as the warrior, the natural world in all its dimensions as well as the human, can liberate, enrich, sustain and transform the client's relationships with self and God. *[Article copies available for a fee from The Haworth Document Delivery Service: 1-800-HAWORTH. E-mail address: <docdelivery@haworthpress.com> Website: <http://www.HaworthPress. com> © 2004 by The Haworth Press, Inc. All rights reserved.]*

KEYWORDS. Gender, nature, plurality, co-creation, patriarchy

[Haworth co-indexing entry note]: "Liberating Images of God." Stone, Cynthia. Co-published simultaneously in *American Journal of Pastoral Counseling* (The Haworth Pastoral Press, an imprint of The Haworth Press, Inc.) Vol. 7, No. 2, 2004, pp. 1-11; and: *The Image of God and the Psychology of Religion* (ed: Richard Dayringer, and David Oler) The Haworth Pastoral Press, an imprint of The Haworth Press, Inc., 2004, pp. 1-11. Single or multiple copies of this article are available for a fee from The Haworth Document Delivery Service [1-800-HAWORTH, 9:00 a.m. - 5:00 p.m. (EST). E-mail address: docdelivery@haworthpress.com].

http://www.haworthpress.com/web/AJPC
Digital Object Identifier: 10.1300/J062v7n02_01

The construction of images of God, like the construction of images of self and other, arises from a mix of interpersonal relationships, cultural context, language, and the personal unconscious. Like the image of the idealized parent, or ego ideal, the image or images of God held consciously or unconsciously are repositories of ultimate value and meaning. While most psychotherapy chooses to avoid dealing directly with images of God (Goldberg, 1996), pastoral counselors are in a unique position to relate to and assist in the transformation of God images, which are inevitably connected to self images.

New understandings of ourselves and our world that emerge from quantum theory and the paradigm shift out of the rational, scientific, mindset of the Enlightenment send us searching for new images of God and ourselves. The legacy of the Enlightenment has been both a restriction in images of God and an abandonment of the attempt to discover, define, or experience anything called 'God' at all. As Armstrong notes "The idea of a personal God seems increasingly unacceptable at the present time for all kinds of reasons: moral, intellectual, scientific and spiritual" (1993, p. 396). Instead, she continues "Since the 1960s, there has been a fresh interest in mysticism, expressed in the enthusiasm for Yoga, meditation and Buddhism, but it is not an approach that easily consorts with our objective, empirical mentality" (Ibid, p. 397). While people who come for pastoral counseling may be more inclined toward having an image of a personal God, they, as well as those who no longer find 'God' a useful concept in their lives, could benefit from an exploration and transformation of the images of God they hold or reject.

Quantum theory moves us from a worldview that is mechanistic, static, closed and linear to a wider horizon that is holistic, dynamic, open and non-linear (O'Murchu, 1992). The paradigm shift, of which quantum theory is a part, reclaims the irrational, imaginative, mystical dimension of life. Philosophers like Huston Smith and Ken Wilbur have looked to the East to reveal dimensions of human experience beyond those countenanced by modern Western rationalism. These further dimensions of experience center primarily on expanded awareness of the transcendental source of being and of transformed awareness of one's own being. The implication for our practice as pastoral counselors is not to guide clients to satori or samadhi. There are other experts for that, but we can use the implications of an infinitely expanded awareness of God's presence, which echoes the awareness of mystics of all faiths, to expand and liberate the God images of our clients with the goal of more abundant life.

Spiritual and psychological growth always involves necessary losses. Clients usually present at a time of disequilibrium, sometimes longing to restore a previous state of well-being or in a state of pain and confusion because the previous situation, relationship, job, understanding, image of God is now revealed to be inadequate. There is no going back, but the way ahead is not clear either. This is an opportunity for spiritually sensitive clinicians to listen not only for the reliving of family of origin issues, unresolved interpersonal or intrapsychic conflicts, narcissistic deficits, and biochemical issues, but for the presence of unrecognized images of God manifesting in the client's waking and dreaming life. Presenting problems in relationships or in self-esteem are an indication of a need to listen more deeply to need for healing and wholeness in the person's life which, from the point of view of a spiritually sensitive clinician, inevitably involves some expression of a larger Spirit at work, no matter how disguised or disavowed.

Two particular restrictions on God images are relevant here. Both are legacies of the patriarchy that has dominated the history of God in all traditions since about 1500 BC (Armstrong, 1993). One has to do with gender and the other has to do with non-anthropomorphic images of God in nature. Both restrictions are embedded in a world view that is literal, empirical, dualistic, category bound and hierarchical. It is a world view that claims to have access to 'objective' reality and universal truth, known by experts who mediate that knowledge to the lay public. While this view is still robust in fundamentalist communities of all faiths, residues linger in the less conscious domains of our own and our clients' lives. Living as we do in a time of transition, with one foot in the old order and one foot in the new, we can find ourselves full of contradictions, e.g., speaking of gender in stereotypical ways while knowing gender is multiple and fluid or speaking of God as a personal being while knowing that God can be understood as a way of being, as a verb, energy or emptiness. Both/and paradoxes are the hallmark of the new understanding and can be brought to bear in our clinical practice as we accept both feet of our clients, the one in the old order while encouraging the other one to enter or stay in the new order.

This approach is also based on the understanding that we all have choices about how we view the world as well as how we act in the world. Instead of seeing God as the creator of all to whom we must appeal for mercy and intervention, we can co-create with God (whatever 'God' has come to mean for us) through our imagination that becomes the source of our actions in the world.

GENDER

Gender has traditionally been understood as determined by anatomy. Mary Hawkesworth, a feminist academic, tells the story of going to a family reunion in the summer of 1996. She told her nephew she was using her sabbatical to write a book on gender. Her "sixteen-year-old nephew quipped, 'There are men and there are women. What more is there to say? Short book'" (1997, p. 649). Unfortunately many people still think like Hawkesworth's nephew. There is a need to clarify that gender is not anatomy. Gender is a social construction that then becomes a determining factor in the organization of the society in which it has been constructed (Flax, 1990). Gender may or may not be congruent with anatomy, sexual identity, sexual behavior and social role (Hawkesworth, 1997). Some feminists claim there is an essence to femininity which echoes but re-values depreciated cultural stereotypes of women as connected and nurturing. However, increasing awareness of diversity and philosophical questioning that we can know the 'essence' of anything, leads to a vision of greater plurality and flexibility in the concept of gender no matter what the anatomy is. In fact, this understanding extends the tradition of Freud's awareness of our innate bisexuality and Jung's construct of the animus and anima and the union of opposites. In these days, we might say we have many aspects of ourselves, or multiple selves that can have more than one implication for our gender identities.

Much work has been done in the past thirty years by feminist psychoanalysts (e.g., Chodorow, Benjamin, Dimen, Flax), by researchers into women's development (e.g., Gilligan, the Stone Center, Belenkey et al.) by feminist theologians (e.g., Johnson, Chopp, Schussler Fiorenza, Reuther) and the burgeoning feminist spirituality movement to rewrite misogynist images of women and to reclaim feminist images of God. There is still much work to be done to build upon and expand these challenges to the patriarchal tradition and integrate these new understandings into our own work and practice and the lives of our clients. One aspect of this work has to do with the gendered experience of the self in relation to a gendered God image. The ability to image God as both male and female and ourselves as male or female in relationships to God in all the forms this might take is a form of abundance for both men and women. However, since both we and our clients are a long way from being able to play in imagination and prayer in full freedom and delight with the full range of gender possibilities in relation to God images, I will focus on some beginning and clinically relevant possibilities of expansion.

Many, but not all, women and some, but not many men, have made progress in imaging God as a Mother who nurtures, comforts and guides. The qualities of nurturance, comfort and guidance are socially approved feminine qualities and it does not take much of a shift to experience them in relation to a God image, especially as most traditions already have such images of the feminine divine. For example, in Judaism, the *Shekinah* or presence of God, *Ruach* or breath of God and *Hesed* or the womb (compassion) of God are feminine words. In Christianity, Julian, Origen, Ambrose and Gregory of Palmas, among others wrote of Jesus as a mother as well as father. In Buddhism, there is *Tara*, the *bodhisattva* of compassion, like the female version of *Kwan Yin*. Looking at images of God in the Torah and in the writings of early Christian theologians, there was a freedom to imagine that has been lost in the Enlightment centuries of logical correctness. For example, Gregory of Palmas writes "Christ . . . nurses us from his own breast, as a mother, filled with tenderness, does with her babies." The freedom to imagine intimate body contact with a Divine image is an important resource for spiritual life, but one which most of our clients have difficulty allowing themselves to do, no matter what the genders of their God images are. In this regard, it might be easier, for example, for a man to approach a feminine image of God for imaginative holding and comfort than to image a man, as it would be for a woman who has had abusive experiences with men.

There has been less progress in recognizing and claiming aspects of a feminine God that are not nurturing. Less stereotypical feminine qualities exist, but are not easy to find in the Judeo-Christian tradition. The Hebrew leader, Judith, is inspired to seduce and then murder the enemy of her people, Holofernes. With the understanding that images are metaphors, not game plans, Judith, like Joan of Arc in the Christian tradition, can be seen as warriors for God and in their initiative, strength and determination, images of God's presence in these more assertive activities. They are, of course, not sanctions for 'holy war' or activities that harm others. The Hindu image of Durga, the goddess who successfully slays the demon, understood as an inner state of bondage, is a more useful, but less culturally available image. Likewise, the ferociousness of the Buddhist Kali in destroying the manifestations of ignorance as to our true nature as Buddha nature is appreciated in Eastern cultures, but absent from our own.

Some women clients are afraid of their own anger and potential strength, which they experience as destructiveness. One such client presented a dream image of a terrifying man whom she felt was intent on destroying her. Summoning up her own courage in the therapy hour, and at the suggestion of the therapist, she was able to confront this image and ask what it wanted. In her imagination the image dissolved into a weeping child and brought her in touch with her own woundedness. In daring to approach the terrifying male image, she was drawing on the image of God within her, the strength, courage, daring to face the 'enemy.' One could say the threatening man, the image of evil, was destroyed. One could also say that to the degree she connected with herself in the image of God's strength and compassion the image of the evil enemy was revealed to be her own hurt and helpless self. It is important to recognize that many states exist within a client: not only the wounded, helpless self, and the angry, destructive self, but also the image of God, the powerful, compassionate and wise self.

Although God language was not used directly with this client, I have often invited clients who are receptive to talking about their God images to imagine themselves as God in a particular difficult situation. One could also invite clients to imagine what a good parent would do in this situation, or to imagine being a good parent themselves, but for people who hold conscious god images which are the repositories of ultimate value, transformation has to be experienced at this level for it to make a real difference in the client's meaning system. For example, a man who had been part of an evangelical, fundamentalist community was making the slow and painful evolution out of this community to a more autonomous sense of self and a life that felt fuller and freer for himself. However, he still had a very restricted image of God as a punitive, judging father who would be severely critical and demand some sort of penance for a misdeed. Imagining how he would be as God, while initially evoking all sorts of resistance, led to a connection with far greater compassion and forgiveness than evidenced by his previous God image.

Expanding images of God to include female as well as male, non-stereotypical feminine as well as the traditional feminine are, perhaps, as far as we can go with counseling clients, with the exception of those who are gay, lesbian or bisexual who might have an easier time imaging God in same-sex, embodied, sexual ways. The goal with all clients is to support their continuing evolution, which, in terms of God images means supporting the expansion and transformation of their God image, beginning where they are and progressing according to their pace. The therapist, however, needs to be aware of the possibilities and opportunities to invite a fuller experience of the divine.

NATURE

It has been my experience that clients invariably point to nature as the source of their experiences of God. This has surprised me especially among those who attend religious services regularly and would have been expected to have more anthropomorphic images of God such as those discussed above. The difference seems to be in personal experience as contrasted with images inherited from a tradition. Paying attention to a client's own experience of peace, joy, love, radiance and transcendence can offer important clues about what the God image is for the person. One disturbed teenager from a wealthy, but alcoholic, family told me she was only at peace when she was riding her horse. Perhaps that experience gave her some solitude and/or a glimpse of the Buddhist experience of 'at-one-ness' with her horse and her ride. Another client recalls the image of the sun shining through trees in the summer when she walked from church to her grandmother's house. It was that image from nature rather than the church service that stayed with her as revealing God's presence. That image is now a resource to her in adulthood. Similarly, a man who is currently a Roman Catholic priest, traces his relationship to God to the experience as a boy of sitting in the hollow of an old Douglas Fir tree which had been scarred by lightening. The tree provided a refuge from a chaotic family situation and became his God image. On a recent visit to this childhood refuge, he discovered the tree was no longer standing. He now feels it has become part of him, as he like the tree has been scarred by lightening, hollowed out and is a refuge for others.

Nature, the earth, the human body and sexuality have been devalued along with women in the Western patriarchal tradition. Feminist spirituality has taken the lead in reclaiming images of God in gardening and the seasons as metaphors for the sacredness of our human lives and deaths. Native American spirituality honors the sacred in totem animals and holy ground. In Hindu and Tantric spirituality, sexuality is an expression of the sacred. The Hebrew tradition finds God in the mountains, wind, fire and water. The eagle, the bear, the stag and the dove are God images. Christianity is more restrictive, tending, at least in modern times, to limit God images to Father, Son and Holy Spirit. The Holy Spirit, however, has many possibilities for imaginative expression, the classical ones being the dove or the wind. Medieval Christian women mystics, Meister Eckhardt, and Matthew Fox celebrate God in creation and draw upon multiple images from nature. Finding images of God in nature can become further developed in an experience of oneness with nature, which is called nature mysticism. While nature mysticism is a commonly understood experience and goal in Eastern religions, there is an unfortunate view in some parts of the psychoanalytic community that nature mysticism occurs when object relations are disappointing (Lalene Rector in 12/7/01 lecture). If one accepts this view, one applies a reductionist and Enlightenment stance to a phenomenon that is widespread, non-pathological and a source of actual or potential renewal for clients who may also have good object relations. Ken Wilbur (2001) places nature mysticism in developmental line of spirituality beyond the interpersonal and psychological realm. It is, in his understanding, the first level of the transpersonal or transcendent consciousness. In American literature, Thoreau and Whitman are prime examples of nature mysticism.

Given the religious pluralism which has permeated this country, clients may be familiar with the reverence for nature in Native American spirituality and the nature mysticism of Eastern religions. Clients may, if invited, be able to describe their 'holy ground,' a particular place that makes them feel grounded, centered and perhaps aware of or connected to, or one with a sense of the sacred, immanent or transcendent. Going there in reality or imagination offers a clearing in the world of pressing concerns. It can become a place where the deep inner self of the client can emerge and be identified as either true self or a God image. Contact with this level of self and God experience is a source of growth and transformation.

Nature, of course, is not always gentle or benign. Destructive natural events such as lightening strikes, floods, earthquakes and life-threatening wildlife do not easily evoke images of God. They may, in fact, evoke images of evil and raise questions about the bad things that can happen to good people. Different religions have offered different stories to account for the dark side of nature and of life. It is useful to explore the understandings clients have of why bad things happen and what images of God they use. As therapists, we would want to question the Judeo-Christian legacy, now muted, that bad things are punishments for bad deeds. Taking a quantum theory approach to both natural and human events, we can see both the interdependence of events and the human inability to control the way the universe works. We would, perhaps again like the Hindus, see the blend of creation and destruction in all of life and see it as a whole.

WORKING WITH IMAGES

Clinicians who are comfortable with images and have experienced image work themselves, might invite clients into contact with their sacred images whether it is a dialogue with a God image personified as male or female, or into felt contact with a sacred place, tree or animal. Allowing time in the session for such an imaginative experience, or suggesting this as an exercise between session and then asking for some sharing of the experience can yield significant therapeutic results. In an encounter with his or her construct of the Holy, a client can feel loved and valued in a deeper way, or such an encounter can reveal the fear, sense of inadequacy, shame and unworthiness that the client is struggling with. One is then in a position to assess how much of this sense of unworthiness is due to limited or harmful God images.

Traditional psychotherapy has worked in the realm of the rational mind to perceive and understand emotions and less rational phenomena such as images and dreams. In recent years, attention has been paid to biological factors leading to the recognition of biochemical disorders requiring medication. Now, as we move into a new paradigm, we can begin to approach the spiritual realm where images and intuitive sense are the primary modes of knowing rather than logic and empirical verification.

Techniques like dream amplification, dialogue with wisdom figures (cf. Progoff), and guided imagery are useful in the process of image expansion and transformation. In dream amplification one uses a Jungian approach and invites the dreamer to change the dream or end it in a new way. One can also take the part of any image in the dream and speak as if the dreamer were this image or allow this image to speak to the dreamer. Dialogue can occur in imagination between a client and his or her image of God. It is important to listen to what God says and discern whether what the client reports appears to be valid wisdom in the line of any spiritual tradition or whether it is a non-helpful misunderstanding or residue of a tradition that is constrictive, e.g., teachings that illness is a punishment, that homosexual behavior is sinful, that women are of less value than men, etc.

Guided imagery is initiated by the counselor with the permission of the client and leads the client to the holy place and encounter of their choice. Again, one provides the safety and space for the encounter and listens careful to the report, attending to the wisdom it holds for the client's current situation.

In work with God images that offers the possibility of expansion and transformation, one does not have to avoid or criticize constricting or punitive images of God. Instead of approaching a client's God images from a rational, empirical base, one can rest on the foot in the new paradigm, creating a bridge for the client to shift their weight from the old to the new way of understanding and experiencing their God. And, as I have been suggesting, this new way is more flexible, inclusive, multiple and fluid. It invites clients to be more imaginative in co-creating their lives in partnership with a plurality of God images, which can enrich and sustain them.

REFERENCES

Armstrong, Karen (1993). *A History of God*. New York: Ballantine Books.

Belenky, Mary Field, Blythe McVicker Clinchy, Nancy Rule Godberger, and Jill Mattuck Tarule (1986). *Women's Ways of Knowing: The Development of Self, Voice, and Mind*. New York: Basic.

Benjamin, Jessica (1988). *The Bonds of Love: Psychoanalysis, Feminism, and the Problem of Domination*. New York: Pantheon.

Chodorow, Nancy J. (1989) *Feminism and Psychoanalytic Theory*. New Haven, Conn: Yale University Press.

Chopp, Rebecca S. (1991). *The Power to Speak: Feminism, Language, God*. New York: Crossroads.

Dimen, Muriel (1997). "The Engagement Between Psychoanalysis and Feminism." *Contemporary Psychoanalysis* 33(4):527-548.

Flax, Jane (1990). *Thinking Fragments: Psychoanalysis, Feminism & Postmodernism in the Contemporary West*. Los Angeles: University of California Press.

Gilligan, Carol (1982). *In a Different Voice*. Cambridge, MA: Harvard University Press.

Goldberg, Constance (1996). "The Privileged Position of Religion in the Clinical Dialogue." *Clinical Social Work Journal*, vol. 24, no. 2, pp. 125-136.

Hawkesworth, Mary (1997). "Confounding Gender." *Signs: Journal of Women in Culture and Society* 22(3):649-685.

Johnson, Elizabeth A. (1994). *She Who Is: The Mystery of God in Feminist Theological Discourse*. New York: Crossroads.

O'Murchu, Diamuid (1992). *Our World in Transition: Making sense of a changing world.* Lews, Sussex: Temple House.

Progoff, Ira (1975). *At a Journal Workshop.* New York: Dialogue House Library.

Reuther, Rosemary Radford (1986). *Women-Church: Theology & Practice.* San Francisco: Harper & Row.

Schussler Fiorenza, Elisabeth (1989). *In Memory of Her: A Feminist Theological Reconstruction of Christian Origins.* New York: Crossroads.

Wilber, Ken (2000). *Integral Psychology: Consciousness, Spirit, Psychology, Therapy.* Boston: Shambala.

Attachment, Well-Being, and Religious Participation Among People with Severe Mental Disorders

Michele A. Schottenbauer, PhD
Roger D. Fallot, PhD
Christine L. Tyrrell

SUMMARY. Traditional mental health models have frequently asserted that religious participation among those individuals with severe mental disorders is either harmful or a manifestation of their illness. Newer research, however, has found that this is not always the case. The current study examined the relationship between attachment states of mind and religious participation among a sample of consumers diagnosed with severe mental illness at a community mental health agency. We found a correspondence between attachment states of mind and participation in religious activities. Specifically, consumers who preferred interpersonal closeness with others reported a higher frequency of prayer, church service attendance, and scripture reading than those who preferred interpersonal distance. Our results suggest that people who

---

Michele A. Schottenbauer is affiliated with The Catholic University of America. Roger D. Fallot is affiliated with Community Connections. Christine L. Tyrrell is affiliated with Onondaga Case Management Services, Inc.

[Haworth co-indexing entry note]: "Attachment, Well-Being, and Religious Participation Among People with Severe Mental Disorders." Schottenbauer, Michele A., Roger D. Fallot, and Christine L. Tyrrell. Co-published simultaneously in *American Journal of Pastoral Counseling* (The Haworth Pastoral Press, an imprint of The Haworth Press, Inc.) Vol. 7, No. 2, 2004, pp. 13-25; and: *The Image of God and the Psychology of Religion* (ed: Richard Dayringer, and David Oler) The Haworth Pastoral Press, an imprint of The Haworth Press, Inc., 2004, pp. 13-25. Single or multiple copies of this article are available for a fee from The Haworth Document Delivery Service [1-800-HAWORTH, 9:00 a.m. - 5:00 p.m. (EST). E-mail address: docdelivery@haworthpress.com].

prefer a particular interpersonal distance from humans also maintain a similar relationship with their God-object. *[Article copies available for a fee from The Haworth Document Delivery Service: 1-800-HAWORTH. E-mail address: <docdelivery@haworthpress.com> Website: <http://www.HaworthPress.com> © 2004 by The Haworth Press, Inc. All rights reserved.]*

KEYWORDS. Interpersonal closeness-distance, prayer, research, scripture reading, states of mind, mental health agencies

While religious activity and beliefs among people with severe mental disorders have often been viewed as harmful, recent research has shown that religion may also have a constructive role in the lives of people with severe mental disorders (Fallot, 2001; Koenig, Larson, & Weaver, 1998). One framework for understanding participation in religious activities in this population is Kirkpatrick's (1999) theory of the relationship between attachment styles and religious behavior. While Kirkpatrick's theory has the power to explain positive religious involvement among people with severe mental disorders, empirical examinations of the model have been limited to nonclinical samples. The current study sought to explore the potential relationship between attachment and religious behavior in a sample of people diagnosed with severe mental illnesses.

Kirkpatrick (1999) has built a theory of religious participation and behavior on the attachment theories of Bowlby (1969/1982) and Ainsworth (1985). According to Kirkpatrick, perceived relationships with God meet the defining criteria of attachment relationships according to Bowlby and Ainsworth in several ways. For instance, prayer and worship may serve the function of seeking and maintaining proximity to an attachment figure, while turning to religion in times of crisis may be related to perceptions of God as an attachment figure who can provide a safe haven. Other religious attitudes, such as the belief that God watches over people, show that God may be viewed as a secure base for exploration of the environment.

Growing out of Kirkpatrick's (1994) theory of attachment and religion are two main hypotheses: the compensatory and correspondence theories (Granqvist, 1998; Granqvist & Hagekull, 1999; Kirkpatrick, 1999). The correspondence hypothesis holds that a person's quality of relationship with God is similar to the quality of relationships they have with other people. The compensatory hypothesis, in contrast, states that a relationship with God functions to make up for what people lack in their relationships with other humans.

Studies have reported empirical evidence consistent with both the correspondence and compensatory hypotheses. For instance, research has found that secure attachment is related to more positive images of God (Kirkpatrick, 1998; Kirkpatrick & Shaver, 1992), and that adult attachment security is related to a better perceived relationship with God (Granqvist & Hagekull, 2000; Kirkpatrick, 1998). Moreover, secure adult attachment style has been found to be related to greater faith maturity (TenElshof & Furrow, 2000). Security of attachment has been connected to strong links between social relationships and expression of religiosity, as well as a tendency to develop increasing conviction in religious standards over time (Granqvist & Hagekull, 1999). Some data indicate that the correspondence between attachment and relationship with God are directly linked to one's relationship with parents. For instance, Granqvist (1998) found that transmission of religiosity along generational lines was stronger among secure respondents.

Some studies, however, have pointed towards the compensatory hypothesis. For instance, Granqvist and Hagekull (2000) found that single people are more religiously active than those in a romantic relationship. Dickie et al. (1997) have argued that God becomes a "substitute attachment figure" as children separate from parents with age, or when fathers are absent from the home, and the work of Lovinger, Miller, and Lovinger (1999) has lent support to the idea that religion may be used by adolescents to repair problematic attachments. Overall, studies have repeatedly shown that insecure attachment styles have been related to greater and more sudden changes in spiritual beliefs during adulthood than secure attachment styles (Granqvist, 1998; Granqvist & Hagekull, 2001; Granqvist & Hagekull, 1999; Kirkpatrick, 1997a).

Previous studies linking attachment and religious beliefs have used measures of adult attachment styles. The current study assesses adult attachment states of mind, as measured by the Adult Attachment Interview (George, Kaplan, & Main, 1985). The constructs of attachment styles and attachment states of mind share a conceptual framework, i.e., a theoretical relationship to Ainsworth's (Ainsworth et al., 1978) original three categories of infant attachment: secure, insecure-avoidant, and insecure-ambivalent. Despite sharing this conceptual framework, there are key differences between the constructs of attachment style and attachment states of mind that lead to different operationalizations. Specifically, attachment style is assumed to be accessible to conscious awareness and is measured by subjects' self-report of their own approach to current relationships. Attachment states of mind are thought to reflect individuals' internal working models of attachment that are governed by unconscious rules and can only be assessed through detailed discourse analysis as individuals talk about their thoughts and feelings in relationship to early attachment figures. Both methods result in subjects being placed in attachment categories. Attachment styles tend to refer to the categories of secure vs. insecure, with two insecure categories labeled insecure-ambivalent and insecure-avoidant (Ainsworth et al., 1978). Attachment states of mind tend to refer to categories of autonomous vs. nonautonomous, with two non-autonomous categories labeled as preoccupied (hyperactivating) and dismissing (deactivating).

One might expect that there would be a strong relationship between attachment styles and attachment states of mind, but this expectation has not been supported by the empirical literature (Waters, Merrick, Albersheim, & Treboux, 1995). Therefore, it seems important to distinguish between previous studies linking attachment styles to religious behavior and the current study. Individuals with autonomous states of mind have been described as "free to evaluate" attachment (Main & Goldwyn, in press). Their descriptions of attachment experiences are minimally influenced by defensive processes and therefore interviews with autonomous individuals tend to be coherent and well integrated. Many studies have found that individuals with autonomous states of mind have greater ego resiliency and more effective emotion regulation than individuals with nonautonomous states of mind (e.g., Kobak et al., 1993; Kobak & Sceery, 1988). Individuals with more deactivating styles tend to maintain more distance in relationships (Kobak et al., 1993; Kobak & Sceery, 1988), while more hyperactivating individuals admit to more emotional distress and engage in greater self-disclosure with others (Dozier, 1990; Dozier & Lee, 1995).

The current study assesses the link between religious behavior and attachment states of mind in a population of individuals with severe psychiatric disorders. While the correspondence and compensatory hypotheses have been tested in a wide range of populations, no studies have been conducted among people with severe mental illnesses. In fact, until recently a common belief in psychiatry was that religious expression among those with severe mental disorders is frequently a sign of or contributor to their illness, especially among those with psychotic disorders such as schizophrenia (for a review, see Fallot, 2001). Recent research has suggested that religion may also have a constructive role in the lives of people with severe mental disorders (Fallot, 2001; Koenig,

Larson, & Weaver, 1998), but these studies have not examined the relationship of attachment and religious participation in this population.

The current study hypothesized that among people with diagnoses of severe mental disorders, more autonomous and less deactivating attachment states of mind would be related to increased religious activity participation, including religious service attendance, prayer, and reading scripture. We also sought to explore two alternative hypotheses. The first alternative hypothesis is that, in this population, the strongest correlation of participation in religious activities is severity of dysfunction. For instance, consumers with the most severe functional impairments, those who are severely depressed, or those who feel a general lack of value in their lives may not have the energy or motivation to participate in religious activities. These difficulties may override the effects of attachment on their religious behaviors. The second alternative hypothesis is that diagnosis is related to participation in religious activities. Specifically, consumers with schizophrenia or schizoaffective illness may be more preoccupied with religious ideation as part of their illness and therefore may demonstrate a disproportionate number of religious behaviors when compared to those with affective illnesses.

METHOD

Participants

The sample consisted of 43 participants with serious psychiatric disorders, including schizophrenia or schizoaffective disorder (67.4%) and major depression or bipolar illness (32.6%). Participants were recruited from the consumers receiving comprehensive case management services at a private, not-for-profit mental health agency in Washington D.C. The sample was 62.8% female and predominantly African American (69.8%), with 30.2% Caucasian. Participant age at interview ranged from 23 to 63 ($M = 40.67$, $SD = 8.02$). Many participants were never married (44.2%). The average level of education was 11.79 years ($SD = 2.10$). In the last year, 60.4% were unemployed, had irregular work, or were retired; 35.0% held full-time or regular part-time employment or were students.

The sample was fairly religious, with 76.7% reporting that they were "sure God really exists and knows me." Overall, they were comparatively active in religious activities, reporting engaging in these activities once a month or more: going to church (55.8%), praying (85.7%), and reading scripture (59.5%). Most respondents described themselves as currently having a Protestant affiliation (67.4%). Other religions represented included Roman Catholic (16.3%), Jewish (7.0%), Islamic (4.7%), Non-Denominational Christian (2.3%), and None/Agnostic (2.3%).

Procedure

Each participant was interviewed twice. The first interview included the Adult Attachment Interview (AAI) and demographic questions, along with measures of working alliance, quality of life, and depression. Participants separately completed an interview that addressed questions about their participation in religious activities. Information about the participants' diagnoses and clinicians' assessments of their general levels of functioning were collected from mental health records.

Measures

Interviewers asked participants for demographic information, including gender, age, ethnicity, and employment in the past year. They also asked participants how religious they were and how important religion was to them. Participants were also asked the frequency with which they attended church services, prayed, and read scripture.

Attachment states of mind. Attachment states of mind were measured by the AAI (George et al., 1985) in semistructured interviews individually administered to each participant by Christine L. Tyrrell, at the time a graduate student at the University of Delaware. The AAI includes questions about relationships with parents during childhood and specific memories. The interview questions were made more concrete for this population. For instance, the question "Why do you think your parents behaved as they did during your childhood?" was broken down into "You said your parents were [participant's description]. Why do you think that they were that way?"

Attachment interviews were coded using a modified version of Kobak's (1989) Q set, which includes two dimensions: deactivating (vs. hyperactivating) and autonomous (vs. nonautonomous). The Q set was developed based on Main and Goldwyn's (in press) classification system for the AAI, which classifies individuals into one of three primary attachment states of mind: autonomous, dismissing (deactivating), or preoccupied (hyperactivating). Good concordance rates have been found between the Q set and Main and Goldwyn's system (Kobak et al.,

1993); however, there are a few important differences between the two systems. The classification of participants into Main and Goldwyn's state-of-mind categories is based on how individuals discuss their attachment, not on the nature of the experiences themselves. The original Q set was designed to have 100 items that describe both aspects of the interviewee's attachment state of mind, as well as aspects of the interviewee's attachment experience. In the present study, the original Attachment Q Set was modified to include only 46 state-of-mind items, thus making the assessment more consistent with Main and Goldwyn's assessment. Using the dimensional Q set rather than the categorical system allowed for increased power and reliability.

For the modified Q set, two criterion Q sorts were generated, one for the deactivating (vs. hyperactivating) attachment dimension and another for the autonomous (vs. nonautonomous) dimension. Criterion sorts were generated by Roger Kobak and Tyrrell, with interrater reliability of .90 for both dimensions. Each participant's distribution on the 46 items was then correlated with the corresponding 46 items of two criterion Q sorts, resulting in two correlation coefficients for each participant. These coefficients were then converted to z scores and used in analyses. Participants whose individual distributions produced positive correlations with the deactivating prototype were characterized by a dismissal of attachment, limited access to memories, and idealization of attachment figures. Participants whose individual distributions obtained negative correlations with the deactivating prototype were characterized by preoccupation with attachment issues and evidence for unresolved conflict with parents. Positive correlations with the autonomous prototype were associated with coherence, access to specific memories, and objective perspective on early relationships. Negative correlations with the autonomous prototype were associated with incoherence and lack of objectivity about early relationships. More information about the Q-sort procedure can be found in Kobak et al. (1993).

Tyrrell coded all AAI transcripts. She was trained at a 2-week workshop given by Mary Main and Erik Hesse and passed reliability testing, obtaining agreement of at least 80% with Main and Hesse. Approximately 20% of manuscripts were Q-sorted by other coders, all of whom had attended Main and Hesse AAI coding workshops. Interrater reliability, computed as Pearson correlations, was .65 for the participant sample. The interrater reliability expected on the basis of chance is approximately 0 for the Attachment Q Set. This level of interrater reliability is similar to that reported in other studies using the original Attachment Q Set (e.g., Dozier et al., 1994; Kobak et al., 1993).

Quality of life. The Quality of Life Interview (Lehman, 1988) measures relationship, quality of life, and general well-being on 7-point Likert-type scales ranging from 1 (terrible) to 7 (delighted). Interviewers asked participants to give objective descriptions of family and social relations and then to subjectively rate their satisfaction with each domain. Participants also rated overall life satisfaction. Objective and subjective ratings have been found to have acceptable internal consistency (Lehman, 1988). Higher levels of overall life satisfaction have been found to be related to less depression and anxiety among people with severe mental illness (Lehman, 1988).

Depression. Depression was measured by the short form of the Beck Depression Inventory (BDI; Beck et al., 1961). The short form of the BDI consists of 13 statements that focus on depressive symptoms, including fatigue, sadness, and guilt. Participants rated how the degree to which statements reflected their feelings during the past week. The short form of the BDI has been shown to correlate very highly with the standard form and has been shown to have quite good internal consistency (Gould, 1982; Reynolds & Gould, 1981).

Client diagnoses. Participant diagnoses were obtained from their records.

General level of functioning. The General Assessment of Functioning (GAF; American Psychiatric Association, 1994) provides a method for measuring clients' overall psychological, social, and occupational functioning. Clinicians rated each participant's level of functioning using the GAF every 6 months and evaluations completed during the most recent year were averaged to provide a measure of overall functioning. Interrater reliability for the GAF has been found to be adequate (Edson et al., 1997).

RESULTS

Autonomous (vs. nonautonomous) attachment states of mind were significantly associated with frequency of church service attendance, personal prayer, and scripture reading (see Table 1). Deactivating (vs. hyperactivating) attachment states of mind were significantly inversely associated with frequency of prayer. The relationship between autonomous attachment states of mind and frequency of prayer was significantly larger than the relationship between deactivating attachment states of mind and frequency of prayer ($t = 2.98$, $p < .01$). There was a

TABLE 1. Correlations Between Attachment States of Mind and Religious Activities

Religious Variables	Attachment States of Mind		*t*
	Autonomous (vs. nonautonomous)	Deactivating (vs. hyperactivating)	
Frequency of Church Service Attendance	.30+	−.24	1.86
Frequency of Prayer	.43**	−.39*	2.98**
Frequency of Reading Scripture	.43**	−.22	2.29*

+$p < .10$. *$p < .05$. **$p < .01$.

similar significant difference for frequency of scripture reading ($t = 2.29$, $p < .05$).

Correlations between measures of overall functioning with religious activity participation were calculated to rule out the hypothesis that only higher-functioning clients would be able to participate in religious activities (see Table 2). Results showed no significant correlations between global functioning, depression, or quality of life and religious activities. This supports the hypothesis that attachment states of mind, not general level of functioning, are related to greater participation in religious activities.

Differences between diagnostic groups were explored on a variety of measures in order to examine the hypothesis that certain religious activity participation levels or attachment styles would only exist for a particular diagnostic group. There were no significant differences between the schizophrenia/schizoaffective disorder group and the affective disorder group on measures of global functioning, $t = −.44$, $p = .66$, depression, $t = −.93$, $p = .36$, or global quality of life, $t = 1.12$, $p = .27$. Similarly, there were no differences between groups on measures of importance of religion, $t = .50$, $p = .62$, or religious activities such as church service attendance, $t = −.79$, $p = .44$, prayer, $t = −.92$, $p = .36$, or reading scripture, $t = −.42$, $p = .68$. There were differences between groups, however, in attachment states of mind. Participants in the schizophrenia/schizoaffective disorder group tended to have less autonomous (vs. nonautonomous) attachment states of mind ($M = −.28$, $SD = .41$) than those in the affective disorder group ($M = .01$, $SD = $

TABLE 2. Correlations Between Measures of Overall Functioning and Religious Activities

Religious Variables	Measures of Overall Functioning		
	Global Functioning	Depression	General Quality of Life
	(GAF)	(BDI)	(QOL)
Frequency of Church Service Attendance	.08	.18	−.04
Frequency of Prayer	.06	.22	−.11
Frequency of Reading Scripture	−.02	.12	−.06

.49), $t = -1.97$, $p = .056$, but no differences existed between deactivating (vs. hyperactivating) attachment states of mind for the two groups.

CONCLUSIONS

The current study supports the hypothesis that attachment states of mind are related to participation in religious activities among people with severe mental disorders. Specifically, the results support a correspondence between attachment states of mind and religious activities, in that more autonomous and hyperactive attachment styles were associated with more religious activities while nonautonomous and deactivating attachment styles were associated with fewer religious activities. Deactivating states of mind are associated with maintaining interpersonal distance from others, whereas hyperactivating states of mind are associated with being preoccupied with attachment relationships (Kobak et al., 1993; Kobak & Sceery, 1988). Our results suggest that people who tend to prefer interpersonal distance from humans also maintain such a distance with their God-object.

Autonomous states of mind are associated with freedom to evaluate attachment bonds nondefensively, with nonautonomous states of mind associated with the lack of this capacity (Main & Goldwyn, in press). Our data indicate that people with severe mental illness who are more able to evaluate freely their attachment bonds are more likely to engage in both social religious activities such as church services and solitary religious activities such as prayer. This relationship between autonomous attachment and religious activities in people with severe mental disorders provides one way of understanding how religious involvement can at times be associated with positive adjustment in this population.

The results indicated no support for two alternative hypotheses. First, these data indicate that attachment states of mind are related to participation in religious activities while measures of overall functioning, depression, or quality of life are not. Thus, our findings do not support the hypothesis that, in this population, those who have less severe impairments will participate in more religious activities. Second, our data indicate that a variety of diagnostic groups participate relatively equally in religious activities. We found no support for the hypothesis that religious participation is significantly more frequent among those diagnosed with schizophrenia or schizoaffective illness.

Overall, the current study supports the hypothesis that among people with severe mental disorders, interpersonal attachment states of mind correspond to levels of religious activity participation. The next questions to be addressed include whether attachment also affects the *quality* of religious participation, and how clinicians may distinguish between positive and less positive religious participation among consumers.

REFERENCES

Ainsworth, M. D. (1985) Patterns of attachment. *Clinical Psychologist, 38*, 27-29.

Ainsworth, M., Blehar, M., Waters, E., & Wall, S. (1978). *Patterns of attachment: A psychological study of the strange situation.* Hillside, NJ: Erlbaum.

American Psychiatric Association. (1994). *Diagnostic and statistical manual of mental disorders* (4th ed.). Washington, DC: Author.

Beck, A. T., Ward, C., Mendelson, M., Mock, J., & Erlbaugh, J. (1961). An inventory for measuring depression. *Archives of General Psychiatry, 4*, 53-63.

Bowlby, J. (1988). *A secure base: Parent-child attachment and healthy human development.* New York: Basic Books.

Dickie, J. R., Eshleman, A. K., Merasco, D. M., Shepard, A., Vander Wilt, M., & Johnson, M. (1997). Parent-child relationships and children's images of God. *Journal for the Scientific Study of Religion, 36*, 25-43.

Dozier, M. (1995). *Attachment states of mind among case managers in different models of case management.* Unpublished manuscript.

Dozier, M., Cue, K., & Barnett, L. (1994). Clinicians as caregivers: Role of attachment organization in treatment. *Journal of Consulting and Clinical Psychology, 62*, 793-800.

Dozier, M., & Lee, S. (1995). Discrepancies between self- and other-report of psychiatric symptomatology: Effects of dismissing attachment strategies. *Development and Psychopathology, 7*, 217-226.

Edson, R., Lavori, P., Tracy, K., Adler, A., & Rotrosen, J. (1997). Interrater reliability issues in multicenter trials: Part II. Statistical procedures used in Department of Veterans Affairs Cooperative Study #394. *Psychopharmacology Bulletin, 33,* 59-67.

Fallot, R. (2001). Spirituality and religion in psychiatric rehabilitation and recovery from mental illness. *International Review of Psychiatry, 13,* 110-116.

George, C., Kaplan, N., & Main, M. (1985). Attachment Interview for Adults. (Unpublished manuscript, University of California, Berkeley).

Gould, J. (1982). A psychometric investigation of the standard and short form Beck Depression Inventory. *Psychological Reports, 51,* 1167-1170.

Granqvist, P. (1998). Religiousness and perceived childhood attachment: On the question of compensation or correspondence. *Journal for the Scientific Study of Religion, 37,* 350-367.

Granqvist, P., & Hagekull, B. (2001). Seeking security in the new age: On attachment and emotional compensation. *Journal for the Scientific Study of Religion, 40,* 527-545.

Granqvist, P., & Hagekull, B. (2000). Religiosity, adult attachment, and why "singles" are more religious. *International Journal for the Psychology of Religion, 10,* 111-123.

Granqvist, P., & Hagekull, B. (1999). Religiousness and perceived childhood attachment: Profiling socialized correspondence and emotional compensation. *Journal for the Scientific Study of Religion, 38,* 254-273.

Kirkpatrick, L. A. (1999). Attachment and religious representations and behavior. In J. Cassidy & P. R. Shaver (Eds.), *Handbook of attachment* (pp. 803-822). New York: The Guilford Press.

Kirkpatrick, L. A. (1998). God as a substitute attachment figure: A longitudinal study of adult attachment style and religious change in college students. *Personality & Social Psychology Bulletin, 24,* 961-973.

Kirkpatrick, L. A. (1997a). A longitudinal study of changes in religious belief and behavior as a function of individual differences in adult attachment style. *Journal for the Scientific Study of Religion, 36,* 207-217.

Kirkpatrick, L. A. (1997b). An attachment-theory approach to the psychology of religion. In B. Spilka & D. N. McIntosh (Eds.), *The psychology of religion: Theoretical approaches* (pp. 114-133). Boulder, CO: Westview Press.

Kirkpatrick, L. A. (1995). Attachment theory and religious experience. In R. W. Hood, Jr. (Ed.), *Handbook of religious experience.* (pp. 446-475). Birmingham, AL: Religious Education Press, Inc.

Kirkpatrick, L. A. (1994). The role of attachment in religious belief and behavior. In Bartholomew, K., & Perlman, D. (Eds). *Attachment processes in adulthood. Advances in personal relationships, Vol. 5.* (pp. 239-265). Bristol, PA, US: Jessica Kingsley Publishers, Ltd. 342pp.

Kirkpatrick, L. A., & Shaver (1992). An attachment-theoretical approach to romantic love and religious belief. *Personality and Social Psychology Bulletin, 18,* 266-275.

Kobak, R. R. (1989). *The Attachment Interview Q-Set.* (Unpublished manuscript).

Kobak, R. R., Cole, H. E., Ferenz-Gillies, R., Fleming, W. S., & Gamble, W. (1993). Attachment and emotion regulation during mother-teen problem solving: A control theory hypothesis. *Child Development, 64,* 231-245.

Kobak, R. R., & Sceery, A. (1988) Attachment in late adolescence: Working models, affect regulation, and representations of self and others. *Child Development, 59,* 135-146.

Koenig, H. G., Larson, D. B., & Weaver, A. J. (1998). Research on religion and serious mental illness. In R. D. Fallot (Ed.), *Spirituality and religion in recovery from mental illness, No. 80, New directions for mental health services.* (pp. 81-95). San Francisco, CA: Jossey-Bass Publishers.

Lehman, A. F. (1988). A quality of life interview for the chronically mentally ill. *Evaluation and Program Planning, 11,* 51-62.

Lovinger, S. L., Miller, L., & Lovinger, R. J. (1999). Some clinical applications of religious development in adolescence. *Journal of Adolescence, 22,* 269-277.

Main, M., & Goldwyn, R. (in press). Adult attachment classification system. In M. Main (Ed.). *Behavior and the development of representational models of attachment: Five methods of assessment.* Cambridge, England: Cambridge University Press.

McFadden, S. H., & Levin, J. S. (1996). Religion, emotions, and health. In C. Magai & S. H. McFadden (Eds.), *Handbook of emotion, adult development, and aging* (pp. 349-365). San Diego, CA, US: Academic Press, Inc.

Reynolds, W. & Gould, J. (1981). A psychometric investigation of the standard and the short form Beck Depression Inventory. *Journal of Consulting and Clinical Psychology, 49,* 306-307.

TenElshof, J. K., & Furrow, J. L. (2000). The role of secure attachment in predicting spiritual maturity of students at a conservative seminary. *Journal of Psychology & Theology, 28,* 99-108.

Tyrrell, C. L., Dozier, M., Teague, G. B., & Fallot, R. D. (1999). Effective treatment relationships for persons with serious psychiatric disorders: The importance of attachment states of mind. *Journal of Consulting and Clinical Psychology, 67,* 725-733.

Waters, E., Merrick, S.K., Albersheim, L., & Treboux, D. (1995, April). From the Strange Situation to the Adult Attachment Interview: A 20-year longitudinal study of attachment security in infancy and early childhood. In J.A. Crowell & E. Waters (chairs), *Is the parent-child relationship a prototype of later love relationships? Studies of attachment and working models of attachment.* Symposium conducted at the Society for Research in Child Development, Indianapolis, IN.

Concepts of God and Therapeutic Alliance Among People with Severe Mental Disorders

Michele A. Schottenbauer, PhD
Roger D. Fallot, PhD
Susan T. Azrin, PhD
Robert Coursey, PhD

SUMMARY. The current study explored some of the transferential aspects of God representations in a sample of adults diagnosed with severe mental illness. The sample consisted of 100 participants recruited from the consumers who were receiving comprehensive case management services at a community mental health agency. Participants who had positive beliefs about God also tended to have a good working alliance with their case manager, whereas those with more negative beliefs about God tended to have a poorer working alliance. The findings of this study support a common transferential process by which internal object relations form the basis of relationships both with real and transitional ob-

---

Michele A. Schottenbauer is affiliated with The Catholic University of America. Roger D. Fallot is affiliated with Community Connections. Susan T. Azrin is affiliated with Westat, Inc. Robert Coursey is affiliated with the University of Maryland.

[Haworth co-indexing entry note]: "Concepts of God and Therapeutic Alliance Among People with Severe Mental Disorders." Schottenbauer, Michele A. et al. Co-published simultaneously in *American Journal of Pastoral Counseling* (The Haworth Pastoral Press, an imprint of The Haworth Press, Inc.) Vol. 7, No. 2, 2004, pp. 27-39; and: *The Image of God and the Psychology of Religion* (ed: Richard Dayringer, and David Oler) The Haworth Pastoral Press, an imprint of The Haworth Press, Inc., 2004, pp. 27-39. Single or multiple copies of this article are available for a fee from The Haworth Document Delivery Service [1-800-HAWORTH, 9:00 a.m. - 5:00 p.m. (EST). E-mail address: docdelivery@haworthpress.com].

http://www.haworthpress.com/web/AJPC
Digital Object Identifier: 10.1300/J062v7n02_03

jects, i.e., the case manager and God. The implications of these findings for clinical practice are discussed. *[Article copies available for a fee from The Haworth Document Delivery Service: 1-800-HAWORTH. E-mail address: <docdelivery@haworthpress.com> Website: <http://www.HaworthPress.com> © 2004 by The Haworth Press, Inc. All rights reserved.]*

KEYWORDS. Adults, clinical practice, object relations, mental health agencies, transference

Psychoanalytic conceptualizations of the formation and role of God representations have evolved dramatically over the last 100 years. Utilizing the original drive model of personality, Freud understood God representations as projections of the father figure and accompanying feelings about the father. As such, Freud believed that the need for a God representation was a developmentally immature manifestation of neurosis, and would cease with the resolution of Oedipal strivings (Jones, 1996; Meissner, 1984). The theoretical shift offered by object relations and self-psychology theorists, in which the need for relationships is primary, offered a radical rethinking of God representations. God representations moved from the realm of the neurotic to a culturally acceptable avenue for an object-seeking relationship (Guntrip, 1961, 1969; Jones, 1991; Meissner, 1984; Miller, 2000; Rizzuto, 1979).

A variety of object relations theories have been utilized to understand God representations. For instance, Rizzuto (1979) and Meissner (1984) have applied Winnicott's (1953, 1965) theory of transitional objects to God. They argue that a combination of internal (personal) ideas of God interact with external (familial and cultural) concepts of God to create a transitional "God object" which operates between the subjective and objective spheres. Thus, God object representations have strong personal components intermingled with formal and interpersonal elements garnered from one's religion, community, and family.

The personal need for a God representation has also been elaborated by Jones (1991, 1996) and Rector (2000), who have applied Kohut's (1984) theory of selfobject relations to God representations. Kohut (1984) believed that a self develops and is sustained within a selfobject environment, in which certain external objects take on special meanings or functions and become part of internalized, affectively charged relationships that constitute a sense of self. Jones (1991) argues that one's relationship to God participates in this selfobject field, and therefore a God representation is linked to one's sense of self. Rector (2000) applies Kohut's theory of the twinship selfobject relation to God representations. She theorizes that certain Christian beliefs, such as humans being made in the image of God and God becoming human in Jesus, forge a twinship relationship with God that may fill a need to be similar to other beings in the universe.

The strength of these relational approaches is that the mechanisms and defenses that govern normal psychological processes apply also to God representations. Thus, internal objects and the relationships between them, including projective identification, splitting, introjective identification, and other mechanisms, are active components of God representations. God representations then are part of the "transferential ground," and as such are sources of information about a person's object relations (Meissner, 1984; Miller, 2000) and self (Jones, 1991). The concept of transference is used in this paper to refer to consistencies between both internal and external objects and their relationships in a broad sense, rather than in a narrow sense of relationships based on parental images.

The current study explored some of the transferential aspects of God representations in a sample of adults with severe mental illness. Traditionally, many mental health professionals have taken a skeptical view of religious activity and beliefs among people with severe mental illness, considering these beliefs harmful through their likely association with hallucinations, delusions, and rigid adherence to detrimental activities related to religion or spirituality (Fallot, 2001). However, recent research has suggested that religion may also have a constructive role in the lives of people with chronic mental illness, providing additional resources for coping and social support (Fallot, 2001; for a review, see Koenig, Larson, & Weaver, 1998). This multidimensional role of religion among adults with severe mental illness may be related to the types of transference involved. Two theories have been suggested to explain these different functions of religion: the correspondence and compensation theories. The correspondence hypothesis posits that a person's quality of relationship with God is similar to the quality of their relationships with other people, while the compensatory hypothesis speculates that a person's relationship with God compensates for problems with their human relationships (Kirkpatrick, 1999b). Empirical evidence has been found supporting both theories (for a review, see Kirkpatrick, 1999a). This question, however, has not yet been examined among people diagnosed with severe mental disorders.

The current study examined two aspects of object relations theory as applied to God representations. First, we examined the transferential aspect of God representations by comparing God representations to another form of relationship conducive to transference, namely, the relationship of a client to a case manager as measured through the therapeutic alliance. Studies have shown that quality of object-relations have an impact on the therapeutic alliance irrespective of theoretical orientation of the therapy conducted (e.g., Piper, 1991; for a review, see Horvath, 1994). For instance, studies have found that object relations conflicts are enacted in a therapeutic relationship and affect the alliance (Safran, Crocker, McMain, & Murray, 1990). The current study hypothesized that similar qualities of object relations underlie both a client's God representation and the therapeutic alliance with their case manager. This is consistent with the correspondence hypothesis outlined above.

Second, we expected psychiatric diagnosis to be related to quality of God-representations. Rizzuto (1979) found that among neurotic patients, aspects of their God representations were related to certain periods of developmental arrest or difficulty. From a Kleinian perspective, two basic psychodynamic positions underlie various disorders, the schizoid/paranoid position and the depressive position. The schizoid/paranoid position consists of a lack of distinction between inner and outer objects and a use of splitting defenses. It is the precursor to the depressive position, which involves a more mature, integrated self-concept in which it is possible to relate to whole objects (St. Clair, 2000). The current study included clients with schizophrenia/schizoaffective disorders and affective disorders. While these diagnoses do not correspond directly to the schizoid/paranoid and depressive positions, they do capture a relative severity of impairment which may involve different defenses, and therefore, different transferences. It was hypothesized that the God representation would correlate more strongly with therapeutic alliance for the schizophrenia/schizoaffective disorder group than the affective disorder group for two reasons. First, the schizophrenia/schizoaffective disorder group was expected to show stronger signs of splitting, and therefore show a clearer distinction between good and bad object representations. Second, it was hypothesized that the affective disorder group would have more integrated internal object relations, and therefore be able to relate to their case manager in a more mature, realistic way, so that the actual relationship would predominate.

METHOD

Participants

The 100 participants were recruited from the consumers who were receiving comprehensive case management services at a private, not-for-profit mental health agency in Washington D.C. About half the clients approached agreed to be interviewed and completed the interview. Reasons for declining to participate included inability to complete the 90-minute interview in one to three sessions, participant's hospitalization, participant's refusal to come to the agency, and lack of interest.

The sample was 62% female and predominantly African American (69%), with 28% Caucasian and 3% reporting other ethnicities. Participant age at interview ranged from 23 to 68 years ($M = 40.96$, $SD = 8.56$). Most participants were single (61%) or separated or divorced (29%), with 6% married, 3% widowed, and 1% living with a significant other. The average level of education was 11.71 years ($SD = 2.83$). In the last year, 58% were unemployed, had irregular work, or were retired; 37% held full-time or regular part-time employment or were students.

Participants had an identified Axis I diagnosis of either Schizophrenia or Schizoaffective Disorder (66%) or an affective disorder (29%). Over half had a formal substance abuse or dependence diagnosis (59%), with individual case managers reporting a larger percent (67%) as having substance abuse or dependence problems. The age at first psychiatric hospitalization ranged from 10 to 52 years ($M = 25.14$, $SD = 8.63$). Almost half (43%) had a major medical problem in addition to psychiatric or substance abuse problems.

The sample was fairly religious, with 77% reporting that they were "sure God really exists and knows me." Most respondents described themselves as currently having a Protestant affiliation (63%). Other religious preferences represented included Roman Catholic (23%), Islamic (4%), Non-Denominational Christian (3%), Jewish (3%), and None/Agnostic (3%).

Measures

Demographics. An initial demographic questionnaire included items on gender, ethnicity, and marital status. Questions about education and employment in the last year were asked later in the interview. Information about number of lifetime hospitalizations and age of first hospitalization were collected from the case manager with participant consent.

Beliefs about God. Beliefs about God were measured by a 30-item scale consisting of statements of beliefs about God or a higher power (see Table 1). Items in the scale were developed specifically for individuals with severe mental illness (Fallot, 1996). Participants rated statements on 5-point Likert-type scales ranging from "disagree" to "agree." The scale was factor-analyzed into a forced-choice two-factor solution using principal component analysis and Varimax rotation with Kaiser normalization on the full 100 participant sample. Twenty-six of the 30 items loaded strongly on one factor, resulting in a Positive Beliefs about God subscale and a Negative Beliefs about God subscale (see Table 1). Examples of items from the Positive Beliefs about God subscale include "accepts and understands me just as I am," "is a healing power in my life," and "is very patient and slow to be angry with me." Items from the Negative Beliefs about God subscale include "punishes people who sin," and "will condemn me to eternal punishment if I do not believe the right things or live a good life." Items that did not load on a factor included "controls everything that happens to me," "is very strict about the right way for me to live," "seems more like a mother than a father to me," and "seems more like a man than a woman to me." Reliability for the subscales was good, with Cronbach's alpha .91 for the Positive Beliefs about God subscale and .71 for the Negative Beliefs about God subscale.

Working alliance. The Working Alliance Inventory (WAI; Horvath & Greenberg, 1989) is a 36-item client-therapist inventory adapted here to the case management relationship. The WAI was developed and validated based on Bordin's (1976) assertion that working alliance is a distinct concept from unconscious projections; thus, the WAI was designed to measure actual collaboration with the therapist (Horvath, 1994). The WAI has successfully been adapted to the case management relationship for adults with serious mental disorders in a number of studies (e.g., Calsyn, Morse, & Allen, 1999; Neale & Rosenheck, 1995; Ralph & Clary, 1992; Tyrrell, Dozier, Teague, & Fallot, 1999). Respondents are asked to indicate responses on a 7-point Likert-type scale ranging from "never" to "always" to questions such as "I feel uncomfortable with [name of current case manager]" and "I feel confident in [name of current case manager]'s ability to help me." For the purposes of the present study, only the total score was utilized. The WAI has been shown to have good reliability and validity (Horvath & Greenberg, 1989; for a review, see Horvath, 1994).

TABLE 1. Beliefs About God Scale Items

Subscale	Items (I believe that God or a higher power:)
Positive Beliefs	is like a father who loves us
	wants only the best things for my life
	accepts and understands me just as I am
	saves me from my sins and errors
	has a special purpose in mind for me
	values and appreciates my unique talents and gifts
	forgives me whenever I do something wrong
	is a source of great help to me
	is like a close friend to me
	comforts me when I am upset
	is patient and slow to be angry with me
	is all powerful in my life
	is a healing power in my life
	is very close personally to me
	guides and directs every step of my life
	is really on my side in times of trouble
	frees me from my worries and burdens
Negative Beliefs	punishes people who sin
	will condemn me to eternal punishment if I do not believe the right things or live a good life
	doesn't really care what happens to me
	is easily angered by some of the things I do
	leaves me on my own to work out any difficulties I might have
	remembers every mistake I make and counts each one against me
	is too busy to be bothered by my concerns
	is just a "crutch" I would be better off without
	is not really able to make much of a difference in my life
Items not included	controls everything that happens to me
	seems more like a mother than a father to me
	seems more like a man than a woman to me
	is very strict regarding the right way for me to live

Procedure

Interviews were conducted as part of a mental health agency's self-evaluation. Interviews were conducted by a clinical psychologist, a graduate student, and a team of eight supervised research assistants.

RESULTS

Positive and negative beliefs about God, working alliance, and lifetime hospitalizations did not differ between the psychiatric disorder categories (see Table 2). For all participants, positive beliefs about God were associated with a better working alliance ($r = .31$, $p < .01$), whereas negative beliefs about God were associated with a poorer working alliance ($r = .22$, $p < .05$). While these trends were present in both diagnostic categories, the correlations were only significant for participants diagnosed with schizophrenia or schizoaffective disorders, not for the group with affective disorders (see Table 3). However, the correlation between positive beliefs about God and working alliance in the schizophrenia/schizoaffective disorder group was not significantly different than the same correlation in the affective disorder group ($z = .94$, n.s.). Likewise, the correlations between negative beliefs about God and working alliance in the two diagnostic categories were not significantly different ($z = .76$, n.s.).

Separate hierarchical regressions were conducted on the WAI for schizophrenic/schizoaffective and affective disorders (see Table 4). The first step included lifetime hospitalizations as a rough estimate of the severity of the mental illness. For participants with schizophrenia/schizoaffective disorders, the number of lifetime hospitalizations did not significantly predict the quality of the working alliance. Beliefs about God significantly predicted the working alliance above and beyond lifetime hospitalizations. For participants with affective disorders, lifetime hospitalizations significantly predicted the working alliance; however, beliefs about God did not add significantly to the prediction of the variance.

CONCLUSIONS

The findings of this study support a common transferential process by which internal object relations are consistent with relationships both with real and transitional objects, i.e., the case manager and God. Participants who had positive beliefs about God also tended to have a good working alliance with their case manager, whereas those with more negative beliefs about God tended to have a poorer working alliance. The transferential nature of God representations is consistent with other empirical literature. For instance, Dickie et al. (1997) found that benevolent perceptions of parents were associated with benevolent percep-

TABLE 2. Comparisons of Beliefs About God, WAI, and Severity of Illness Indicators According to Diagnosis

Variables	Schizophrenia or Schizoaffective Disorder (n = 62)		Affective Disorder (n = 28)		
	M	SD	M	SD	t
Positive Image of God	4.14	.08	4.12	.12	.12
Negative Image of God	2.55	.07	2.79	.12	−1.63
WAI	197.08	34.99	186.11	36.67	1.37
Lifetime Hospitalizations	9.08	7.01	11.56	15.27	−1.05

Note: WAI = Working Alliance Inventory

TABLE 3. Intercorrelations Between Beliefs About God and WAI

Subscale	WAI
Schizophrenia or Schizoaffective Disorder (n = 62)	
Positive Beliefs About God	.37**
Negative Beliefs About God	−.23+
Affective Disorder (n = 27)	
Positive Beliefs About God	.16
Negative Beliefs About God	−.05

Note: WAI = Working Alliance Inventory
+p < .10. **p < .01.

tions of God, regardless of race, socioeconomic status, and religious affiliation of the participants. Likewise, a study of adolescents found that God image was related to both parental communication and self-esteem (Chartier & Goehner, 1976). The general similarity between the findings of these two studies, conducted with non-clinical samples, and the current study, conducted with a sample of clients with severe mental illness, indicates that the psychological processes underlying formation of God images may be relatively independent of mental health status. While the current study only found a significant relationship between God image and working alliance for the schizophrenia/schizoaffective disorder group, it did not find significant differences between the corre-

TABLE 4. Image of God Regressed on WAI, Controlling for Lifetime Hospitalizations

	Step		Model		
	ΔR^2	F	R^2	F	β
Schizophrenia or Schizoaffective Disorder (n = 62)					
Severity Indicator	.01	.27	.01	.27	
Lifetime Hospitalizations					−.07
Beliefs About God	.16	5.11**	.16	3.51*	
Positive					−.18
Negative					.31*
Affective Disorder (n = 27)					
Severity Indicator	.25	7.50*	.25	7.50*	
Lifetime Hospitalizations					−.50*
Beliefs About God	.05	.77	.30	2.96+	
Positive					−.24
Negative					−.02

Note: WAI = Working Alliance Inventory.
+$p < .10.$ * $p < .05.$ ** $p < .01.$

lations for the two diagnostic groups, further supporting this commonality of the transferential process.

Yet, the hierarchical regressions shed some light on how the transferential process may differ according to diagnosis. For the schizophrenia/schizoaffective disorder group, beliefs about God significantly predicted working alliance above and beyond the number of lifetime hospitalizations, a rough measure of severity of functional impairment. This lends support to the hypothesis that the object relations underlying God representations and therapeutic alliance, including defensive mechanisms such as splitting, may have fairly strong impacts on relationships independent of the severity of illness in those affected by schizophrenia/schizoaffective disorders. For the affective disorder group, number of lifetime hospitalizations was a significant predictor of working alliance and God representation did not add to the prediction of the variance. This finding gives initial support to the hypothesis that clients closer to the depressive position may have more integrated object relations and better reality testing, as evidenced by the statistical independence between God representation and therapeutic alliance with the case manager after controlling for severity of impairment.

The current study provided preliminary support for the consistency of psychodynamic processes with quality of God representations among a sample of adults diagnosed with severe mental disorders, thus supporting the correspondence hypothesis. Evidence of defensive processes was inferred by examining the relationship between God representations and therapeutic alliance with a case manager. One weakness of this approach is that quality of object relations was not measured directly. Future studies need to take into account the quality of object relations and defensive processes in order to compare these directly to quality of God image.

As more researchers are exploring the beneficial aspects of including spirituality as a component in the recovery of people with severe mental illness (e.g., Fallot, 2001; Koenig et al., 1998), it is important to link these findings to existing psychological theories. Knowledge of the role of psychodynamic processes in determining the quality of relationships with both real and transitional objects such as God offers insight into the kinds of interventions that could be used in treatment.

REFERENCES

Bordin, E. S. (1976). The generalizability of the psychoanalytic concept of the working alliance. *Psychotherapy: Theory, Research and Practice, 16,* 252-260.

Calsyn, R. J., Morse, G. A., & Allen, G. (1999). Predicting the helping alliance with people with a psychiatric disability. *Psychiatric Rehabilitation Journal, 22,* 283-287.

Chartier, M. R., & Goehner, L. A. (1976). A study of the relationship of parent-adolescent communication, self-esteem, and God image. *Journal of Psychology and Theology, 4,* 227-232.

Dickie, J. R., Eshleman, A. K., Merasco, D. M., Shepard, A., Vander Wilt, M., & Johnson, M. (1997). Parent-child relationships and children's images of God. *Journal for the Scientific Study of Religion, 36,* 25-43.

Fallot, R. (1996). Beliefs about God Scale. Unpublished document. Washington DC: Community Connections.

Fallot, R. (2001). Spirituality and religion in psychiatric rehabilitation and recovery from mental illness. *International Review of Psychiatry, 13,* 110-116.

Guntrip, H. (1961). *Personality structure and human interaction.* New York: International Universities Press.

Guntrip, H. J. S. (1969). Religion in relation to personal integration. *British Journal of Medical Psychology, 42,* 323-333.

Horvath, A. O., & Greenberg, L. S. (1989). The development and validation of the Working Alliance Inventory. *Journal of Counseling Psychology, 36,* 223-233.

Horvath, A. O. (1994). Empirical validation of Bordin's pantheoretical model of the alliance: The Working Alliance Inventory perspective. In A. O. Horvath, & L. S.

Greenberg (Eds.). *The working alliance: Theory, research, and practice.* (pp. 109-128) New York: John Wiley & Sons, Inc.

Jones, J. W. (1996). *Religion and psychology in transition: Psychoanalysis, feminism, and theology.* New Haven: Yale University Press.

Jones, J. W. (1991a). *Contemporary psychoanalysis and religion: Transference and transcendence.* New Haven: Yale University Press.

Jones, J. W. (1991b). The relational self: Contemporary psychoanalysis reconsiders religion. *Journal of the American Academy of Religion, 59,* 501-517.

Kirkpatrick, L. A. (1999a). Attachment and religious representations and behavior. In J. Cassidy & P. R. Shaver (Eds.), *Handbook of attachment* (pp. 803-822). New York: The Guilford Press.

Kirkpatrick, L. A. (1999b). Toward an evolutionary psychology of religion and personality. *Journal of Personality, 67,* 921-952.

Koenig, H. G., Larson, D. B., & Weaver, A. J. (1998). Research on religion and serious mental illness. In R. D. Fallot (Ed.), *Spirituality and religion in recovery from mental illness, No. 80, New directions for mental health services.* (pp. 81-95). San Francisco, CA: Jossey-Bass Publishers.

Kohut, H. (1984). *How does analysis cure?* Chicago: University of Chicago Press.

Meissner, W. W. (1984). *Psychoanalysis and religious experience.* New Haven: Yale University Press.

Miller, M. E. (2000). The interplay of object relations and cognitive development: Implications for spiritual growth and the transformation of images. In M. E. Miller, & A. N. West (Eds.). *Spirituality, ethics, and relationship in adulthood: Clinical and theoretical explorations.* (pp. 307-335). Madison, CT: Psychosocial Press/International Universities Press, Inc.

Neale, M. S. & Rosenheck, R. A. (1995). Therapeutic alliance and outcome in a VA intensive case management program. *Psychiatric Services, 46,* 719-723.

Piper, W. E., Azim, H. R. A., Joyce, A. S., MacCallum, M., Nixon, G. W. H., & Segal, P. S. (1991). Quality of object relations vs. interpersonal functioning as predictor of therapeutic alliance and psychotherapy outcome. *Journal of Nervous and Mental Disease, 179,* 432-438.

Ralph, R. O., & Clary, B. B. (1992, October). *The Working Alliance Inventory: Measuring the relationship between client and case manager.* Paper presented at the National Conference on the State Mental Health Agency Services Research Conference, Baltimore, MD.

Rector, L. J. (2000). Developmental aspects of the twinship selfobject need and religious experience. In A. Goldberg (Ed.), *How responsive should we be?: Progress in self psychology* (Vol. 16, pp. 257-275). Hillsdale, NH: The Analytic Press, Inc.

Rizzuto, A. M. (1974). Object relations and the formation of the image of God. *British Journal of Medical Psychology, 47,* 83-99.

Rizzuto, A. M. (1979). *The birth of the living God.* Chicago: University of Chicago Press.

Safran, J. D., Crocker, P. McMain, S., & Murray, P. (1990). The therapeutic alliance rupture as a therapy event for empirical investigation. *Psychotherapy: Theory Research and Practice, 27,* 154-165.

St. Clair, M. (2000). *Object relations and self psychology: An introduction* (3rd ed.). Belmont, CA: Brooks/Cole Thomson Learning.

Tepper, L., Rogers, S. A., Coleman, E. M., & Malony, H. N. (2001). The prevalence of religious coping among persons with persistent mental illness. *Psychiatric Services, 52,* 660-665.

Tyrrell, C. L., Dozier, M., Teague, G. B., & Fallot, R. D. (1999). Effective treatment relationships for persons with serious psychiatric disorders: The importance of attachment states of mind. *Journal of Consulting and Clinical Psychology, 67,* 725-733.

Winnicott, D. W. (1953). Transitional objects and transitional phenomena. *International Journal of Psycho-Analysis, 26,* 137-143.

Winnicott, D. W. (1965). *The maturational process and the facilitation environment.* New York: International Universities Press, 1965.

The Subjective Experience of God

M. Chet Mirman, PhD

SUMMARY. A theory of the psychological basis for the experience of God is presented which represents a dialectical resolution of the debate between theists and atheists. The present paper argues that the experience of God is essentially a form of projection and as such is an internal event that does not exist independent of an individual's psyche. Nevertheless, belief in God is thought to be a compelling and entirely natural phenomenon that human beings are innately inclined to experience. A distinction is made between faith in a particular belief–namely, faith in the existence of a loving, omnipotent God–and an *attitude of faith*. It is suggested that belief in God, while not essential for an attitude of faith, can serve to foster such an attitude, which is, in turn, the basis for experiences of transcendence. *[Article copies available for a fee from The Haworth Document Delivery Service: 1-800-HAWORTH. E-mail address: <docdelivery@haworthpress.com> Website: <http://www.HaworthPress.com> © 2004 by The Haworth Press, Inc. All rights reserved.]*

KEYWORDS. "Attitude of faith," atheist, dialectical, projection, psychology, theist, transcendence

---

M. Chet Mirman is a clinical psychologist in private practice. He is Assistant Professor at the Illinois School of Professional Psychology/Argosy University-Northwest Campus and a founding partner of the Center for Divorce Recovery (E-mail: MCMir@aol.com).

[Haworth co-indexing entry note]: "The Subjective Experience of God." Mirman, M. Chet. Co-published simultaneously in *American Journal of Pastoral Counseling* (The Haworth Pastoral Press, an imprint of The Haworth Press, Inc.) Vol. 7, No. 2, 2004, pp. 41-54; and: *The Image of God and the Psychology of Religion* (ed: Richard Dayringer, and David Oler) The Haworth Pastoral Press, an imprint of The Haworth Press, Inc., 2004, pp. 41-54. Single or multiple copies of this article are available for a fee from The Haworth Document Delivery Service [1-800-HAWORTH, 9:00 a.m. - 5:00 p.m. (EST). E-mail address: docdelivery@haworthpress.com].

Belief in God is so old and so widespread that one might be tempted to conclude that so many billions of people can't all be wrong. But might the ubiquitousness of this enduring belief reveal more about human nature than about the nature of God? It is the thesis of this paper that the experience of God results from the projection of an internal image out onto the external world. A part of one's self-system is experienced as not only separate from one's self, but as something which the self stands in relationship to. This phenomenon can be a normal (as opposed to abnormal or pathological), natural (as opposed to supernatural) and healthy (as in emotionally and spiritually growthful) internal event, but it is an internal event nonetheless.

Four related concepts coalesce to form the basis for the present paper. The first is the belief that human beings universally yearn for experiences of transcendence, that is, they yearn to be free from the constraints of security-oriented ego activity. The second is the fact that, for some, belief in a powerful, benevolent god can help to facilitate such experiences of transcendence. The third is the notion that human beings are "hard-wired" with a propensity to have a sense of self, as well as a sense of God–or something God-like–and that these two innate propensities are intrinsically interconnected. And the fourth is the hypothesis that individuals with well-developed egos tend to have experiences of transcendence that are psychologically similar to a theist's experience of transcendence but which the theist would describe as "an encounter with God."

WHAT IS GOD?

It is difficult to define or even describe God, and in fact, the mystical branches of the great religions have long insisted that to do so is to diminish God (Cooper, 1997; Armstrong, 1993; Watts, 1951). Mystics who have written about their experiences of the divine claim that to have an experience of God is to know something that cannot be perceived through the senses, comprehended through logic, or adequately described through language. It is argued here that the ineffability of these experiences of God is a result of the fact that God is a literary, rather than a scientific, concept. As such it is simply not amenable to the same rules of logic that apply to phenomena like planets, molecules or photosynthesis.

To describe an "encounter" with God is to focus on the contents of one's psyche. The experience that the individual has of God is a literary description of a subjective experience–that is, of a particular type of internal representation that is the object of that individual's attention. It is also a description of the significance and meaning that that experience has for that person, and its implications for his experience of the world. To an empiricist, for whom only observable phenomena or conclusions that are inductively derived from such observations are seen as real, such notions may seem childish or pathological. Nevertheless, it is a way of describing a subjective experience that is meaningful to those who either speak the same language (i.e., who share the same metaphysics), or know how to translate or interpret such literary descriptions of one's inner experience. Much like dreams, the God being described here is a human creation. It is a projection of human processes from within one's psyche and onto the external world that contains a wealth of information about the individual, and so, like dreams, should be taken seriously. But to take an experience of God seriously is not the same as taking it literally, that is, as a factual account of a real phenomenon in the world that exists independent of one's psyche.

Despite the mystics' claims of the ineffable nature of God, there do, nevertheless, appear to be some fairly universal beliefs about the nature of this reified projection that is universally referred to as God. These are summarized in the American Heritage Dictionary (1972), which defines God as: " A being of supernatural powers . . . believed in or worshipped by a people . . . conceived as the perfect, omnipotent, omniscient originator and ruler of the universe."

The similarity between this idealized characterization of God and the way that an infant experiences his parents is unmistakable. Accompanying both of these experiences of the "parental" other is a complementary sense of self. Standing in relationship to the perfect, omnipotent, omniscient "parent" is a self that is experienced as helpless, needy, weak and relatively powerless. The longing to return to such a dependent state is universal because of the appeal of being taken care of by a loving, powerful parent and the sense of well-being that accompanies such an experience. This parental God can only be experienced when one's sense of self is in a complementary state of childish receptivity. To quote the New Testament (Luke 18:17): "Truly, I say to you, whosoever does not receive the Kingdom of God like a child shall not enter it" (Schiller, 1994).

THE YEARNING FOR TRANSCENDENCE

The yearning to return to a younger, non-defensive way of being–to recapture lost innocence, to experience awe, wonder and a sense of the sacred, and to feel the sense of being part of something larger than one's own "skin-encapsulated 'I'" (Watts, 1969)–is universal. On the other hand, our daily, work-a-day, secular lives are governed to a large extent by the need to anticipate and plan for the future and to guard against danger. We tend to think strategically, and to experience things (including people) as means to other ends. On an intra-psychic level most of us are dominated most of the time by what Harry Stack Sullivan (1953) referred to as "security operations," the ego's responses to perceived threats to the self-system. This vigilance, however, comes at a cost. The ego defenses that have developed in order to protect against trauma to one's sense of self override other important human capacities in much the same way that our fight-or-flight system overrides lower priority systems when we are facing physical danger. And in much the same way that our "fight-or-flight" system can become a chronically activated system (Bensen, 1975/2000), these protective security operations come to operate even when the sorts of dangers that the system evolved to protect against are not present. This conflict between the need for strong ego controls and the yearning to "regress" to more primitive ways of being is a struggle that is a universal part of being a human being.

In his classic book, *I and Thou*, Martin Buber (1958/1970) addressed this dichotomy of possibilities when he wrote: "The world is twofold for man in accordance with his twofold nature." In our ordinary consciousness we see the world as composed of "Its," that is, objects to be used as means to some end. There is a logic to this determined world. Stripped of the childlike qualities that produce a sense of awe and wonder, this is a soul-less world that is orderly, predictable, understandable, and to a considerable extent, controllable. It is the world of science, engineering and commerce. But it is also the world of Maya, the Hindu term for the compulsive pursuit of illusions based on the false hope that we can control our destinies and find a life of permanent security and contentment, a life that is free of pain and suffering (Watts, 1969). In short, it is the ego-based illusion that we can, in the end, achieve victory over nature. According to Buber, the world of I-It is necessary for survival, but it is insufficient for a full life: "without It a human being cannot live. But whoever lives only with that is not human."

The second form of consciousness that Buber refers to is the world of I-Thou relationships. According to Buber, "Man lives in his spirit when he is able to respond to his (Thou). He is able to do that when he enters into this relation with his whole being." This involves a quality of consciousness that was captured in a poem by the British poet William Blake (Schiller, 1994):

To see a World in a grain of sand,
And a Heaven in a wild flower

This way of experiencing one's self in the world was referred to by Abraham Maslow (1968) as B-Cognition, the consciousness of Being (in contrast to D-Cognition, the consciousness of Doing). B-Cognition is a form of consciousness that is available once one's lower order, but higher priority, needs (e.g., needs for food or for safety) have been sufficiently taken care of. Unencumbered by lower level demands, the individual is free to let go of his defensive, instrumental posture toward the world and attend to higher order concerns. Love, rather than survival and security, takes center stage.

Maslow (1964) described a number of characteristics of what he labeled "peak experiences," the spiritual, transcendent moments that self-actualized individuals are able to have. They include: (1) the transcendence of dichotomies and polarities leading to a sense of the entire universe as an integrated and unified whole, (2) a nonjudgmental, accepting mode of cognition, (3) perceptions that are relatively free from distortions based on the biases that our own needs and agendas create, resulting in the ability to see something in its own Being, that is, as an end in itself, (4) a disorientation in time and space creating a sense of universality and eternity, (5) a sense of the sacredness of all things, (6) a sense of wonder, awe, reverence and humility before the greatness of one's experience, (7) a loss of fear, inhibition and defensiveness, (8) the individual feeling himself to be a free agent making conscious choices that are his, (9) feeling more loving toward others, (10) feeling less needy, less striving and less selfish.

We all long to transcend the defensive inhibitions that restrict the range and depth of our experience, and keep hidden our deepest, most authentic selves. For some, experiences of transcendence are life's deepest and most meaningful moments, and so these experiences are fostered and actively pursued. Such individuals consciously seek out what Mihaly Csikszentmihalyi (1990) referred to as experiences of "flow" through their involvement in contemplative activities like prayer or meditation, or in artistic activities such as painting, writing or music.

Others, living lives of "dis-ease" and caught up in the futile and illusory pursuit of security, yearn for relief. They suffer from what could be termed "ego-fatigue" and seek experiences that allow them to rest their chronically stressed egos. Getting drunk, using drugs, and engaging in passive, "escapist" activities like spending long hours playing video games or watching television, are examples of commonly chosen activities of relief. While the activities in the latter group are obviously not the same as the I-Thou experiences described by Buber, or the peak experiences described by Maslow, they share in common the relaxation of ego security operations. It should be pointed out that these two modes of functioning are not entirely mutually exclusive. Consider, for example, a jazz musician who is high on heroin that he uses to escape from the pain of his life. It is conceivable that he could, at the same time, have an experience playing his instrument that could be described as ego transcending as he "loses himself in the music." That is, though he is obviously creating the music that he is playing, his subjective experience of the process is that it feels to him as though he is being carried by the music, music which seems to have a life of its own and which feels as though it is creating itself. Thus it feels as if he is merely a vehicle for the expression of this music. The experience of immersion in this process is accompanied by a relative lack of attention to one's self and thus also, by relief from ego security operations.

TRANSCENDENCE AND FAITH IN GOD

At the heart of all transcendent experiences is an *attitude of faith*. An attitude of faith is the sense of trust or confidence that things will be okay–even without one's vigilant "supervision." This is to be distinguished from faith in a particular belief, such as belief in a loving, omnipotent god. An attitude of faith may involve faith in a particular belief but it does not require it.

An attitude of faith is a derivative of what Erik Erikson (1950/1963) referred to as "basic trust," the result of the successful resolution of the defining challenge of the first stage of psychosocial development. An infant who is reliably comforted and responded to when in need comes to have a sense of the familiar, along with the expectation that what is familiar will be comforting. He begins to trust that his world can be counted on, and that he will be okay. This attitude, according to Erikson, accompanies the infant's first social achievement, the "willingness to let the mother out of sight without undue anxiety or rage, because she has become an inner certainty, as well as an outer predictability. Such consistency, continuity, and sameness of experience provide a rudimentary sense of ego identity. . ."

Later, as an adult, if the individual has an attitude of faith, then he trusts that the world works well and that it will not destroy him even without his active efforts to control events. As a result, he is free to be receptive to the world–both external events and his own inner world of feelings, needs and thoughts. In other words, he does not need to vigilantly watch out for threats to his sense of self because his sense of self does not feel threatened. The security of a strong sense of self allows him to let go of his self, or at least to loosen his grip, because he trusts that it will still be there–undamaged, undepleted and whole–when he returns to it. And so he is less reliant on the security operations that protect his self at the cost of his *spirit* (that is, the mode of Being which, according to Karasu (1999) transforms the ordinary into the extraordinary). Painful emotions that heretofore felt threatening no longer need to be defended against because now they are just seen as painful–painful, but not dangerous or intolerable. And the desperate search for narcissistic supplies to shore up his fragile ego is no longer necessary and can now be seen for the illusory quest that it is.

While an attitude of faith is to be distinguished from faith in a specific belief, it is argued here that faith in the existence of a powerful, loving God whose demands are not only understandable, but are also able to be complied with, can help to facilitate such an attitude. Faith in the belief that by submitting to God's demands one will be, in some sense, taken care of, is a profound comfort with broad ramifications. By adjusting one's posture toward the world so as to be in sync with God's order, the secular dangers that normally occupy one's consciousness lose their power. And with the neutralizing of these dangers the need for security operations dissipates. Free from the need to function in a goal-oriented manner in order to protect one's self, the individual now has the "luxury" of being able to be more child-like again. The experience of awe, wonder and delight, and a sense of the sacred return to consciousness as the world of It is transformed back to a world of Thou, and the need to Do is replaced by the ability to Be.

The reader should note the difference in tone between the present description of faith in God and the more cynical one found in Freud's *The Future of an Illusion* (Freud, 1927/1961). Whereas for Freud "younger" modes of being were seen as psychopathology to be overcome, the ability to "regress" is seen here as a mark of emotional health. Freud wrote that "devout believers are safeguarded in a high degree against the risk of certain neurotic illnesses; their acceptance of the universal neurosis spares them the task of constructing a personal one." He added that "those who do not suffer from the neurosis will need no intoxicant to deaden it. They will, it is true, find themselves in a difficult situation. They will have to admit to themselves the full extent of their helplessness and their insignificance in the machinery of the universe; they can no longer be the centre of creation, no longer the object of tender care on the part of a beneficent Providence.. . . Men cannot remain children forever; they must in the end go out into 'hostile life.'"

STRUCTURAL ORIGINS
OF THE EXPERIENCE OF SELF AND OF GOD

Selfhood is a social construction. According to psychoanalytic theory, particularly the "Object Relations" school (Fairbairn, 1952/1981; Horner, 1979/1982; Kernberg, 1976; Masterson, 1976), as well as more recent social-cognitive theory (Andersen and Chen, 2002), the development of a sense of self begins early in life through the formation of relational schemas. These are internal representations of one's self in relationship to others, mirroring the individual's most significant external relationships. One's sense of self is thus part of a relational matrix in which a particular sense of one's self is accompanied by a complementary sense of the other (or "object") which that self stands in relationship to.

Initially, the infant develops two self-object representational units, a "good" self-object representational unit that feels satisfying and is thus accompanied by positive affect, and a "bad" self-object representational unit that feels punishing and is thus accompanied by negative affect. As the infant's brain continues to develop and the infant experiences a variety of significant interpersonal interactions, these two simple good and bad representational units differentiate into more complex variations. Thus individuals develop a number of self-object representational units, which are then activated according to the interpersonal context that one is in. The particular self-object representational unit that is activated at any given moment becomes the filter through which one experiences one's self, as well as the other(s) that he is engaged with. This process is thus, in part, a form of projection in that we "project" out onto others our interpersonal wishes, fears and expectations.

Consider your experience of your self when you are eating dinner at your mother's home and how this compares to your experience of your self when you are being interviewed for a job or when you are laughing with an old friend. Not only does your experience of your self vary across relationships, but the filter through which you experience others varies as well. In fact, these two complementary components of self-object representational units co-vary with each other. For example, when you are stopped by the police for speeding, the self-object representational unit that is activated might well have as its "object" component (that is, the schema of the other that is projected onto the police officer), a powerful, hostile and frightening parental/father figure. And if this is indeed the activated "object," then chances are good that the complementary self-representation that is activated will be that of a young, vulnerable child who has just been caught misbehaving, and so, feels anxious about "getting into trouble." On the other hand, if you feel deeply loved by someone you idealize, the self-object representational unit that is activated within you may have as its object component a loving, parental figure. And if that is the case, then it is likely that the corresponding self-representation will be that of a young child who feels cared about and safe and thus has a sense of well-being.

The feeling of being loved by an idealized other and the profound sense of well-being and wholeness associated with this experience are core elements of the self-object representational unit that is often described as the experience of communion with God. While being "good" (i.e., behaving morally, exhibiting particular forms of self-control, or overcoming obstacles to achieve certain kinds of personal goals) can help lead an individual to a "state of grace," being "bad" (i.e., having moral lapses, loss of self-control or experiences of failure) tends to trigger the closely related experience of falling from grace or being punished or rejected by God. These two related self-object representational units (i.e., *"good" self-loving idealized other* and *"bad" self-punishing idealized other*) share in common a very young sense of self and an associated object representation that is highly idealized.

It is the yearning to experience one's youngest, most primitive sense of self being loved in an archaic way by an idealized other that sustains these two related self-object representational units and leads to their repeated activation. The apparent irony of the continued activation of the *"bad" self-punishing idealized other* representational unit, despite the primitive yearning for love and the sense of well-being that accompanies it, makes more sense when understood in the following way: This primitive yearning for love is a wish that the individual is unable/unwilling to relinquish. Replacing this primitive self-object representational unit with a more mature one would be a resignation, an acceptance of the loss of the possibility of that form of archaic love. Although this process is an unconscious one, it is as though the individual is saying: "I feel incomplete, but refuse to let go of the hope that I can finally be loved in the kind of way that can make me whole. Because this love can only be experienced while I am in a young self-state, I will cling to archaic self-representations. I will even hold onto self-representations in which I feel that I am 'bad' and which are accompanied by object representations that are punishing and/or rejecting, because despite the immediate frustration of my desire to feel loved, I am thus able to hold onto the hope that if I can just somehow redeem myself I may yet find the primitive love that I yearn for."

EGO DEVELOPMENT AND TRANSCENDENCE

The present article proposes a three stage dialectical model of ego development. Though each is a stage in a developmental process, eventually these stages become distinct ego states that represent different levels of organizational complexity which individuals are then able to move back and forth between. These three stages can be summarized as: (1) a primary ego state, in which the individual functions on a primitive and relatively defenseless level; (2) a secondary ego state, in which the individual is functioning at a more organized, albeit rigid and defensive, manner whereby the central priority is the protection of a fragile sense of self via the use of security operations; and (3) a transcendent ego state, in which the individual's confidence in the stability of his sense of self is sufficiently high that relatively little is needed in the way of security operations to protect and fortify it. It should be noted that, while for purposes of clarification of the nature of these ego states they are being discussed as though they are discrete, mutually exclusive states, in actuality they are three areas on a continuum of states whose boundaries are relatively diffuse.

The primary ego state is characterized by primary process thinking and a sense of awe and wonder toward a world that feels incomprehensible, mysterious and magical. There is a sense of timelessness in which all that exists is the here-and-now. There is a lack of self-object differentiation and a sense of being one with the world. There is also a passive receptivity to one's experiences, an openness to feeling loved and an ability to love. This primary ego state is characterized by the mode of functioning (described above) referred to by Maslow as Being-oriented. On the other hand, lacking the ability to fend for himself, the individual is relatively helpless. This passive stance toward the world is a result of the inability to anticipate the future, to understand causal relationships and the mechanisms and principles by which various phenomena are governed, and to take control and act as an agent who can function in goal-oriented ways to protect one's self. As such the individual in a primary ego state is relatively helpless and vulnerable in the world.

The secondary ego state is essentially a response to the helplessness and vulnerability of the primary ego state. It is characterized by secondary process thinking and a sense of the world as predictable, explainable, controllable and ordinary. There is an awareness of time with considerable focus on the past and the future. There is a sense of one's self as separate from the world. There is also an active, controlling and defensive stance toward one's experiences, and a carefulness in matters of love. This secondary ego state is characterized by a mode of functioning that Maslow referred to as Doing-oriented.

The transcendent ego state, while lacking the helplessness and powerlessness of the primary ego state, has much in common with that state. It is characterized by what the psychoanalyst Ernst Kris (1952) referred to as "regression in service of the ego" in that the mature individual is able to access the primary process thinking that characterizes the primary ego state. There is a sense of awe and wonder toward a world that feels mysterious and magical. There is a sense of timelessness. There is a sense of being part of something larger than one's skin-encapsulated self. There is also a passive receptivity to one's experiences and an openness to feeling loved and to loving. As is the case with the primary ego state, this transcendent ego state is also characterized by a Being-oriented mode of functioning.

Paul Tillich (1952) described anxiety as a reaction to the threat of non-being. The range of phenomena that may be experienced as threatening include experiences of sadness, boredom, emptiness, shame and disappointment. It also includes what Irving Yalom (2002) listed as the four ultimate concerns (note: the term "ultimate concern" was actually coined by Tillich) underlying what he termed "existential anxiety": death, isolation, meaning in life, and freedom. Depending on the early life experiences of the individual and his resulting personality makeup, these vary in the extent to which they are experienced as intolerable and thus a threat to the integrity of one's self.

Individuals in the secondary ego state are organized, in large part, in order to defend against the threat of non-being that a regression to a primary ego state represents. The fear of disintegrating as a result of being a victim of the vicissitudes of one's life leads to the activation of security operations that protect a fragile sense of self. In order to defend against this disintegration the individual adopts a security-oriented stance in which he is instrumental, Doing-oriented, and goal-oriented. Afraid of regressing to the helplessness of the primary ego state, he clings to the security-dominated secondary ego state. Terrified of being weak, vulnerable, and out of control, the individual is apprehensive and mistrustful and so clings to control, all the while wishing that he could let go. This fear-based clinging is essentially the opposite of an attitude of faith and makes the attainment of a transcendent ego state impossible.

The ability to let go, to switch "psychological gears" from a security-oriented mode of consciousness to an open, receptive, non-defensive mode, rests on the degree to which the individual's sense of self feels free from danger or threat. There are essentially two ways that the sense of threat is reduced. While both may (and often do) co-exist, they are distinct approaches and are the basis for two different paths of spiritual development—a humanistic approach and a theistic approach.

The three-stage model of ego development described above is the basis for the humanistic approach. Here, the individual strives to transform his sense of himself, developing a more robust and resilient sense of self via the acquisition of tools to better manage the vicissitudes of life. The individual becomes increasingly competent in, and thus confident about, dealing with his inner world, including painful emotions such as sadness, disappointment and shame. The capacity to manage such experiences lessens the need to defend against what would otherwise feel like threats to selfhood. The sense of fragility and vulnerability that make such a security-oriented, ego-protective stance necessary gives way to an attitude of faith that opens the door to the possibility of experiences of transcendence.

But an *attitude of faith*, and the resulting possibility of transcendence, can also be facilitated by faith in God. The belief that the world has a God-given order to it that is good, and that developing a relationship with God in which one submits to the will of God, can be profoundly liberating. In contrast to the humanistic view that the management of the vicissitudes of one's life is an internal process, belief in God encourages the relinquishing of control to a "higher power." By giving control to God, that is, submitting to the demands of the object representation that is God, the individual is essentially letting go of an ego-based perspective of reality, and thus the need for security operations. The experience of faith in God provides comfort via the activation of a self-object representational unit with an idealized object representation. By subverting one's "selfish" interests to that of God's will, the self-object representational unit that is activated is the *"good" self-loving idealized other* (in contrast to the *"bad" self-punishing idealized other* that is activated by selfish behavior), an experience that is characterized by a profound sense of well-being.

CONCLUSION

Belief in God can be healthy, mature and life-enhancing or it can be unhealthy, immature, and life-negating, the critical element in that determination being not the degree of faith in the belief, but rather the extent to which the belief promotes an *attitude of faith*. An attitude of faith is the basis for the transcendence of ordinary, ego-based consciousness that is preoccupied primarily with the secular concerns of survival and security, as well as derivatives of those needs. Experiences of transcendence, on the other hand, are characterized by the sense of being a part of something larger than one's self, and a sense of awe and wonder toward a world that feels mysterious and magical.

While belief in a loving and powerful God can help to facilitate an attitude of faith, thus opening the doors to experiences of transcendence, so too can the maturing of one's sense of self–with or without a belief in God. As one's sense of self becomes increasingly resilient and the threats to self that existed before come to feel less threatening, the need for protection dissipates, with a resulting relaxation of security operations. Freed from the need to maintain rigid ego control over his functioning, the individual is able to have experiences of "regression" in which he accesses primary process thinking, lives in a world of I-Thou relationships rather than just a world of Its, and is able to Be rather than simply Do. Openness and passive receptivity cease to feel like defenselessness, the hiding of one's vulnerability is replaced by the desire for authentic engagement, and fear and need are replaced by a transcendent sense of the divine.

REFERENCES

Andersen, Susan M & Chen, Serena (2002). The Relational Self: An Interpersonal Social-Cognitive Theory. *Psychological Review*, 109, 619-645.

Armstrong, Karen (1993). *A History of God*. New York: Ballantine Books.

Bensen, Herbert (1975/2000). *The Relaxation Response*. New York: Harper Collins.

Buber, Martin (1958). *I and Thou*. New York: Charles Scribner's Sons.

Cooper, David (1997). *God is a Verb: Kabbalah and the Practice of Mystical Judaism*. New York: Riverhead Books.

Csikszentmihalyi, Mihaly (1990). *Flow: The Psychology of Optimal Experience*. New York: Harper & Row Publishers.

Erikson, Erik (1950/1963). *Childhood and Society*. New York: W.W. Norton & Co.

Fairbairn, W. Ronald D. (1952/1981). *Psychoanalytic Studies of the Personality*. London: Routledge & Kegan Paul.

Freud, Sigmund (1927/1964). *The Future of an Illusion*. Garden City, New York: Anchor Books.

Horner, Althea J. (1979/1982). *Object Relations and the Developing Ego in Therapy*. New York: Jason Aronson.

Karasu, Byram T. (1999). Spiritual Psychotherapy. *American Journal of Psychotherapy*, 53, 143-162.

Kernberg, Otto (1976). *Object Relations Theory and Clinical Psychoanalysis*. New York: Jason Aronson.

Kris, Ernst (1952). *Psychoanalytic Explorations in Art*. New York: International Universities Press.

Maslow, Abraham (1968). *Toward a Psychology of Being*. New York: D.Van Nostrand Company.

Maslow, Abraham (1970). *Religions, Values, and Peak-Experiences*. New York: The Viking Press.

Masterson, James F. (1976). *Psychotherapy of the Borderline Adult*. New York: Brunner/Mazel, Inc.

Schiller, David (1994). *The Little Zen Companion*. New York: Workman Publishing.

Sullivan, Harry Stack (1953). *The Interpersonal Theory of Psychiatry*. New York: W. W. Norton & Company.

Tillich, Paul (1952). *The Courage to Be*. New Haven: Yale University Press.

Watts, Alan W. (1951). *The Wisdom of Insecurity*. New York: Vintage Books.

Watts, Alan W. (1969). *Psychotherapy East and West*. New York: Ballantine Books.

Yalom, Irving (2002). Religion and Psychiatry. *American Journal of Psychotherapy*, 56, 301-316.

Relationship of Gender Role Identity and Attitudes with Images of God

Christina D. Lambert, MA, MEd
Sharon E. Robinson Kurpius, PhD

SUMMARY. After Mass, 282 Catholic attendees at three university Catholic centers completed the Bem Sex Role Inventory, the Attitudes Toward Women scale, and Perceptions of God Checklist. Feminine gender role identity and attitudes toward women predicted images of God as female. Image of God as female was positively related with more nontraditional attitudes toward women, while image of God as male was negatively related to attitudes toward women and positively related to feminine gender role identity. Feminine images of God were positively related to feminine gender role, and masculine images of God were negatively related to attitudes toward women for both men and women. *[Article copies available for a fee from The Haworth Document Delivery Service: 1-800-HAWORTH. E-mail address: <docdelivery@haworthpress.com> Website: <http://www.HaworthPress.com> © 2004 by The Haworth Press, Inc. All rights reserved.]*

Christina D. Lambert is Doctoral Candidate and Sharon E. Robinson Kurpius is Professor, Counseling Psychology, Arizona State University, Tempe, AZ 86287-0611 (E-mail: Christina.lambert@asu.edu).

[Haworth co-indexing entry note]: "Relationship of Gender Role Identity and Attitudes with Images of God." Lambert, Christina D., and Sharon E. Robinson Kurpius. Co-published simultaneously in *American Journal of Pastoral Counseling* (The Haworth Pastoral Press, an imprint of The Haworth Press, Inc.) Vol. 7, No. 2, 2004, pp. 55-75; and: *The Image of God and the Psychology of Religion* (ed: Richard Dayringer, and David Oler) The Haworth Pastoral Press, an imprint of The Haworth Press, Inc., 2004, pp. 55-75. Single or multiple copies of this article are available for a fee from The Haworth Document Delivery Service [1-800-HAWORTH, 9:00 a.m. - 5:00 p.m. (EST). E-mail address: docdelivery@haworthpress.com].

http://www.haworthpress.com/web/AJPC
Digital Object Identifier: 10.1300/J062v7n02_05

KEYWORDS. Attitudes Toward Women scale, Catholic, Bem Sex Role Inventory, image of God, Perceptions of God Checklist

Throughout history, the gods and goddesses of various religions have had dualistic roles and complementary attributes. Schoenfeld and Mestrovic (1991) are among authors who suggest that with the rise of monotheism, the attributes have been collapsed into a multifaceted description for a single male deity. Although they assert that the masculine and feminine are experienced in each gender, accrediting the range of these attributes to a male god legitimizes the superiority of men and the inferiority of women in multiple arenas. According to Johnson (1992), the theistic God is often referred to in male terms and represented as king of the earth. This kingly image, a product of patriarchal systems, validates the continuation of male rulers as the only suitable human role models for such a god-like position. Women, unqualified for kinghood due to their sex, are relegated to subservient roles.

When God is anthropormorphized as father, God is classified as male. Some would argue that God is only symbolically referred to as father to demonstrate proximal relationship rather than to imply the maleness of God. When the image of God is normed on male identity, however, the preeminence of men as godlike is affirmed. On the other hand, women do not find affirmation for their gender role identity as being godlike, but rather there is a sense of otherness or of inferiority (Johnson, 1992). This suggests that women who believe in a male god may internalize their gender role identity as inferior or reject their own gender role identity to be compatible with the identity of God.

Durkheim (1912/1972) asserted that humans have created God in their own image. This perspective was inspired by Feuerbach (1841/1957) who believed that God is an illusion, created by humans. This illusion has both male and female characteristics and roles. Feuerbach and Durkheim's philosophies are known as projection theory, in which individuals view God as they view themselves. Supporting this perspective, Roberts' (1989) study of 185 randomly selected participants from a Midwestern university town found that those who perceive themselves as generous, sincere, and forgiving identified with an image of God as nurturing. Furthermore, Roberts found that those who perceived themselves as suspicious of others viewed God as more disciplining.

Utilizing an attributional theory, Benson and Spilka (1973) suggested that self-esteem influences God-images. Among 128 highly religious adolescent males at a Catholic high school, self-esteem was related positively to loving God images and negatively related to non-loving God images. The authors explained that people maintain images of God that confirm their self-views in order to avoid cognitive dissonance. In this way, both projective and attributional theories are perpetuated by similar self-affirming psychological mechanisms.

Hertel and Donahue's (1995) study of 5th through 9th grade students revealed that girls ($n = 1,340$) were significantly more likely to view God as love in comparison to boys ($n = 1,220$), and boys were significantly more likely to perceive God as authoritarian. While love and authority were perceived as the two primary dimensions for God, Hertel and Donahue also found that both boys and girls emphasized a loving God over an authoritarian God. This supports the findings of Nelsen, Cheek, and Au (1985) who reported that Americans emphasize a supportive image of God.

Contrary to the conclusion drawn by Hertel and Donahue (1995), other researchers have found that male God images prevail over female God images for Americans. For example, analyzing the results of Greeley's Image of God Battery in the 1983 General Social Survey ($n = 1599$), Roof and Roof (1984) found that across Jews and Christians "Creator" was the most dominant image followed by more conventional images and then more personal/contemporary images. Overall, 61% of the respondents indicated that they were "extremely likely" to imagine God as father, while only 25% stated that they would imagine God as mother. When asked, "When you think about God, how likely is each of these images to come to your mind?," the 439 Catholics indicated that their primary images are Creator ($n = 81$), followed by Healer ($n = 68$), Redeemer ($n = 62$), Father ($n = 60$), Friend ($n = 59$), King ($n = 47$), Master ($n = 45$), Judge ($n = 43$), Lover ($n = 41$), Liberator ($n = 39$), Mother ($n = 24$) and Spouse ($n = 17$).

Performing factor analyses of the same data as Roof and Roof (1984), Nelsen et al. (1985) challenged the findings of Roof and Roof. After removing the nontraditional images of spouse, mother and lover, they found that the remaining images fell into two factors, with the five most common images (creator, healer, friend, redeemer and father) comprising the "healer" factor and the four least common (master, king, judge, and liberator) comprising the "king" factor. Consequently, they suggested that there has been a change in Americans' image of God, emphasizing a supportive rather than judging God, especially among women. While Roberts (1989) also found that women were a little more likely to view God as nurturing, he did not find that men were more likely to perceive God as disciplining. Rather, he found that low socio-economic status was more highly related to the perception of God as disciplining.

Vergote, Tomayo, Pasquali, Bonami, Pattyn, and Custers (1969) asserted that the primary image of God is a paternal image, characterized by qualities of knowledge, strength, power, justice, authority, model, law and order, regardless of how individuals perceive themselves. In their study of 60 Catholic high school students and 120 Catholic college students, half male and half female in each group, they found that the image of God was closer to the image of father than of mother. They also found that image of God became more maternal as these students became college students, especially for women.

In another attempt to identify gender images of God, Foster and Keating (1992) completed three studies to evaluate how androcentrism is measured in the Western God-concept. In their first study, they used free response qualitative answers to examine how 93 college students in a lower division psychology course used sex-related terminology to describe God. The majority of the students (87%) used masculine language forms to refer to God, while none of the students referred to God in the feminine. Some students did choose to use inclusive "he/she" pronouns (9%), to indicate God with the pronoun "it" (5%), or not to use pronouns at all (20%).

In their second study (Foster & Keating, 1992), 53 undergraduate students (66% female, 32% male, and 2% unidentified) randomly selected from an introductory psychology population were asked to circle descriptors of God as "male" or "female." Ninety-four percent circled "male" and four percent circled "female." One student chose not to circle either male or female.

In Foster and Keating's (1992) third study, 98 subjects from an introductory social psychology class at the University of Washington were asked to indicate their level of agreement or disagreement with 74 statements about God. One group ($n = 50$) was instructed to answer based on their perception of what most people believed about God, while the other group ($n = 48$) was instructed to answer based on their own perception of God. In the former group, 42 of 50 agreed with God as a "Heavenly Father," nine agreed with God as a "Heavenly Mother," and 31 agreed with "God as a Heavenly Parent." In the latter group, 27 of 48 subjects indicated agreement with God as a "Heavenly Father," 14 agreed with God as a "Heavenly Mother," and 26 agreed with God as a "Heavenly Parent." In their analysis of the Christian students in the former group, Foster and Keating found that Christian students who were willing to consider an image of God as Mother only did so in addition to, rather than as an alternative to, God as Father. Analysis of the latter group suggested that Christian students were reluctant to consider images of God as Mother but were fairly receptive to referral to God as Parent. Regardless, Foster and Keating concluded that the students in their subject pools were generally not trying to describe a gender-neutral parental image of God; rather, they preferred the term "Father," reflecting a specifically gendered (male) parental relationship.

In a qualitative study with 20 undergraduates, Kunkel, Cook, Meshel, Daughtry, and Hauenstein (1999) obtained similar findings. They asked students to provide one to three word responses to an open-ended question about the nature of God (i.e., "What is God like?"). Participants were then asked to perform a card sort with the 85 unique descriptors of God. Traditional male God images (father God) were more salient than female God images (mother God) for college students, even though students identified God as having many feminine gender-related characteristics, such as nurturance. Neither Foster and Keating (1992) or Kunkel et al. indicate their subjects' developmental level. Have their subjects simply accepted the male images of God offered by society or have they questioned and intentionally chosen male images of God?

While Hertel and Donahue (1995) and Nelsen et al. (1985) asserted that supportive images of God are more normative than authoritarian images of God, and Vergote and Tomayo (1981) and Roof and Roof (1984) believed that male God images prevail over female images of God, it is possible that these conclusions are not mutually exclusive. God could be perceived as male and attributed with feminine characteristics. This possibility is supported by Kunkel's (1999), as well as Foster and Keating's (1992) research in which participants viewed God as masculine ("Father" versus "Mother") and both powerful and nurturing.

Since Constantinople (1973) challenged the concept of masculinity and femininity as a single bipolar dimension, researchers (Spence, Helmreich, & Stapp, 1975) have supported the assertion that gender roles are dualistic. Rather than an individual being either masculine or feminine, gender role identity theory posits that both men and women are believed to have both masculine and feminine qualities, varying in degree from individual to individual. Similarly, the masculine and feminine characteristics of God are not mutually exclusive (Schoenfeld & Mestrovic, 1991). Projection theory would suggest that the masculine and feminine gender role identity of an individual positively correlates with the masculine and feminine qualities that an individual ascribes to God.

In addition to gender role identity, gender role attitudes may contribute to images of God. Baker and Terpstra (1986) suggested that the Catholic religion may be less conservative or "orthodox" than the Protestant religions, allowing Catholics to be more receptive toward reconceptualizing the role of women. Similarly, in a longitudinal study of 430 university students at a medium sized, private, nonsectarian, coeducational, midwestern university, Etaugh and Spandikow (1981) found that Catholic religious orientation was one of the characteristics associated with the students who became more liberal in their attitudes toward women. While Rhodes (1983) found that orthodoxy of religion, as defined by exclusion of women from ordination, was positively related to discrimination against women's vocational pursuits, Catholicism was an exception. He suggested that Catholic women might be more progressive than is indicated by their participation in a church that excludes women from ordination.

According to projection theory and gender role theory, it can be argued that there is congruence between an individual's gender role identity and the gender-related characteristics (i.e., powerful vs. nurturing) that the individual attributes to God. That is to say that women and men who identify as highly feminine will be more likely to view God as having feminine qualities. Similarly, women and men who identify as highly masculine will be more likely to view God as having masculine qualities. Furthermore, gender role attitudes may impact traditional or non-traditional images of God.

The purpose of this study was to examine the relationship between Catholic Church attendees' sex and gender-role identity, their attitudes toward women, and their perceptions of God's sex and gender-related characteristics. It was hypothesized that:

H1: Masculine and feminine gender role identities and attitudes toward women will be significant predictors of images of God as male and images of God as female.

H2: Less traditional masculine and feminine gender role identities and attitudes toward women will be positively related to more feminine images of God.

H3: There will be a positive relationship between participants' gender role identities and the gender-related characteristics they attribute to God.

H4: Men and women will differ in their perceptions of God as male, female, masculine and feminine.

METHOD

Participants

Following Mass at Catholic centers at three southwestern universities, attendees were invited to be involved in this study. Although 346 participants returned surveys, 36 surveys were incomplete and could not be included in the data analysis. Another 30 surveys completed by individuals who were not Catholic were also deleted from the data set. The final sample consisted of 282 Catholics attending Mass. Of these 282, 246 were students and 36 were non-students. Therefore, the sample consisted of four groups–three groups of students and one non-student group. The response rate was 90.2%.

Of the total sample, 119 (43.7%) identified as male, 153 (56.3%) identified as female, and ten did not indicate gender. The mean age was 24.15 years (SD = 7.73). Half (50.7%, n = 141) identified as Euro-American, while 23% were Latino (n = 64), 8.7% were Asian-American (n = 27), 6.8% were Filipino (n = 19), 2.9% were International (n = 8), 1 % were Middle-Eastern (n = 3), 1 % were East-Indian (n = 3), .7% were American-Indian (n = 2), and .7% were Pacific Islander (n = 2). Nine participants (3.2%) identified as "other" and four did not identify their ethnicity. Sixty-two majors were represented, including substantial numbers within traditionally male and female dominated fields. Participants were well distributed across academic status: 41 (17.9%) freshmen, 39 (17%) sophomores, 43 (18.8%) juniors, 56 (24.5%) seniors, and 50 (21.8%) graduate students. Fifty-three did not indicate academic status.

All self-identified as Catholic. The mean church attendance was 4.52 times per month (SD = 1.65). The mean for Catholic school education was 6.88 years (SD = 5.94). There were no differences in frequency of church attendance or in the level of agreement with teachings of the Catholic Church across the four groups. The majority of students (66.1%, n = 183) mostly agreed with the teachings of the Catholic church, while 20.9% (n = 58) completely agreed, 11.9% (n = 33) somewhat agreed, and 1% (n = 3) did not at all agree.

Measures

Participants completed a demographic sheet and three assessment devices. The demographic sheet presented questions about age, sex, education, occupations, race/ethnicity, income, level in school, and major. They were also asked about religiosity, orthodoxy, devotionalism and social involvement, and church-related history.

Bem Sex Role Inventory. To ascertain participants' gender identity, they rated themselves on the *Bem Sex Role Inventory* (BSRI; Bem, 1974). The BSRI can be traced to Constantinople (1973), who argued that stereotypically masculine and feminine psychological traits are discrete dimensions and that individuals can possess differing amounts of the two traits in any combination, regardless of the individual's physical gender. In this study, the 30-item short version of the BSRI was used. Ten descriptors are masculine (i.e., independent, assertive), ten are feminine (i.e., affectionate, understanding), and ten are gender neutral (i.e., conscientious, moody). Each descriptor is rated on a seven-point Likert-type scale. Responses are summed within each subscale and then averaged to form total masculinity and total femininity scores, each of which could range from one to seven. The short version generally yields comparable or more reliable scores (alpha ranging from .84 to .86 and from .84 to .87 for masculine and feminine, respectively) than does the 40-item long-form (Bem, 1981; as cited in Campbell & Arthur, 1997). The short form has generally good test-retest and internal consistency reliability, and although the validity data are meager, enough research has been done that the device is promising.

Attitudes Toward Women Scale. Participants also completed Nelson's (1988) 22-item *Attitudes Toward Women Scale-Short* to obtain a measure of their attitudes toward women and their behaviors. This version of the AWS-S uses a five-point Likert-type format with lower scores indicating less agreement with each statement. The 22 items reflect rights and privileges associated with women in regard to vocation, education, marriage, dating and social behavior. Sample statements include "It is all right for men to tell dirty jokes, but women should not tell them." and "A woman should be as free as a man to propose marriage." Scores are summed across items (after reverse coding) and then averaged. Total scores can range from one to five, with lower scores indicating more traditional gender-role attitudes toward women and higher scores indicating strong nontraditional attitudes toward women. Using a national sample, Nelson reported internal consistencies ranging from .78 to .85 across groups classified by age, gender, and socioeconomic status.

Image of God Adjective Checklist. Perceptions of God were assessed with an adjective checklist. The adjectives were selected from the card sort used by Kunkel et al. (1999), based on college student responses to an open-ended question about God's attributes. Items on this scale were clustered to form four subscales based on inter-item correlations: (1) images of God as male; (2) images of God as female; (3) masculine images of God; and (4) feminine images of God. Anthropomorphized items within the checklist were used to constitute the scales of images of God as male (father, brother, and man) and as female (mother, sister, woman).

The last two subscales were compiled from the remaining 79 items on the adjective checklist that had been endorsed as feminine or masculine by six out of eight raters–four male and four female. Two raters were Latino and six were Euro-American. Four were doctoral faculty, four were doctoral students, and one was openly homosexual. The 15 items comprising the feminine images of God subscale included beautiful, comforting, compassionate, gentle, giving, life-giving, listener, loving, nature, nice, peaceful, precious, pure, spiritual, and welcoming. The 20 items comprising the masculine images of God subscale included active, all-knowing, controls our fate, creator, guide, intimidating, judge, lawmaker, life-taker, logical, Messiah, powerful, protector, punishing, relentless, ruler, strong, superior, unafraid, and wise. Forty-four items did not meet the criteria for male, female, masculine or feminine categorization. All items were rated on a scale of one (does not represent God) to four (fully represents God). Items comprising the feminine images of God and the masculine images of God subscales were summed and then averaged. Higher scores on the masculine items reflect more masculine images of God, while higher scores on the feminine items reflect more feminine images of God.

Procedure

At the end of Sunday Mass an announcement was made from the lectern that attendees were invited to fill out a survey on images of God. With one open-ended question, the survey took about 15 minutes to complete. When surveys were returned, participants were thanked and asked if they had any questions. The senior researcher was available to talk with anyone who had questions. Doughnuts were provided.

RESULTS

First, the internal consistencies for the measures of interest were calculated for this sample. The God as male scale, the sum of ratings for the three male anthropomorphized items (man, brother, father) on the adjective checklist, had a coefficient alpha of .50 and a mean of 9.13 (SD = 2.01). The God as female scale, the sum of ratings for the three female anthropomorphized items (woman, sister, mother) had a coefficient alpha of .86, with a mean of 6.93 (SD = 3.11). While satisfactory reliability was achieved with the God as female scale, it was not achieved with the God as male scale. Consequently, all results related to images of God as male should be reviewed cautiously. Next, the masculine images of God and feminine images of God scales were examined. When the 20 items comprising the masculine images of God scale were examined, the Cronbach alpha was .80. The Cronbach alpha for the 15 feminine images of God scale was .84. Finally the internal consistencies for the three gender role identity scales were calculated. For the Attitudes Toward Women scale-Short (Nelson, 1988), the internal consistency for this study sample was .84. When the masculinity and femininity scales of the Bem Sex Role Inventory-Short (Bem, 1981) were examined, the Cronbach alphas were .83 and .88, respectively.

Next, a Chi Square was calculated to determine whether there was a balance between men and women across the four groups. The 2 by 4 Chi Square was not significant. Demographic differences were found among the four groups. There were significant differences in age [F (3, 208) = 7.36, $p < .001$], year in school [F (2, 208) = 4.58, $p = .004$], and family income [F (2, 208) = 3.91, $p = .01$]. No differences were found for parental education. To determine whether these demographic variables were related to the outcome variables, correlations were calculated. Due to the number of correlations and the large sample size, alpha was set at .001. None of the demographic variables were correlated with any of the seven outcome variables. Based on these analyses, it was decided that participants across the four groups could be analyzed as one sample since their demographic characteristics were not related to the outcome measures.

Hypotheses Testing

The first hypothesis predicted that masculine and feminine gender role identities and attitudes toward women will be significant predictors of images of God as male and images of God as female. Two stepwise regressions were conducted to predict images of God as female and images of God as male from participants' scores for masculine gender role identity, feminine gender role identity and attitudes toward women. The results of the first stepwise regression indicated that feminine gender role identity and attitudes toward women account for a significant amount of the variability in images of God as female, $R^2 = .037$, $F (2, 279) = 5.99$, $p = .003$. Attitudes toward women accounted for 2.8 percent of the variance ($\beta = .166$, $p = .005$) and feminine gender role identity accounted for an additional 1.4 percent ($\beta = .119$, $p = .047$). Masculine gender role identity was not a significant predictor of images of God as female. Pearson Product Moment correlations indicated that image of God as female was positively correlated with more nontraditional attitudes toward women, $r = .17$, $p = .003$, and with higher feminine gender role identity, $r = .14$, $p = .008$.

The results of the second stepwise regression indicated that feminine gender role identity and attitudes toward women also accounted for significant variability in images of God as male, $R^2 = .081$, $F (2, 279) = 11.64$, $p < .001$. Together, attitudes toward women ($R^2 = .032$, $\beta = -.215$, $p < .001$) and feminine gender role identity ($R^2 = .043$, $\beta = .217$, $p < .001$) accounted for 7.7 percent of the variance in images of God as male. Masculine gender role identity was not a significant predictor. Examination of the correlations indicated that image of God as male was negatively related to non-traditional attitudes toward women, $r = -.18$, $p < .001$, and positively related to feminine gender role identity, $r = .18$, $p = .001$.

To examine whether participant gender would significantly add to the accounted for variance, hierarchical regressions were conducted. Sex of participant alone was not a significant predictor, $R^2 = .005$, $p = .25$, and when added to feminine gender role identity and attitudes toward women to account for the variance in image of God as female, there was a decrease of .7 percent in the R^2. Next, the ability of gender to enhance the predictive equation for God as male was examined. Again, gender of participant alone accounted for no variance, $R^2 = .00$, and when added to feminine gender role identity and attitudes toward women, it enhanced the accounted for variance by only .9 percent. It appears that sex is not a key variable related to perceptions of God as male or God as female.

The second hypothesis predicted that non-traditional masculine and feminine gender role identities and non-traditional attitudes toward women would be related to more feminine images of God. Stepwise regression was conducted separately for men and women to predict images of God with feminine characteristics from masculine and feminine gender role identities and attitudes toward women. For men, feminine gender role identity ($\beta = .22$ $p < .001$) and attitudes toward women ($\beta = -.11, p = .05$) accounted for a significant amount of the variability in images of God with feminine characteristics, $R^2 = 24.7$, $F(3, 116) = 19.05, p < .001$. Examination of the correlations indicated that for men, images of God with feminine characteristics were positively correlated with feminine (non-traditional) gender role identity, $r = .47, p < .001$. However, the correlation between images of God with feminine characteristics and attitudes toward women failed to reach statistical significance ($r = -.09, p = .18$). As men were more likely to describe themselves as having feminine characteristics they were more likely to ascribe feminine qualities to God.

When women only were examined, only feminine gender role identity ($\beta = .31, p < .001$) accounted for a significant amount of the variability in images of God with feminine characteristics, $R^2 = 9.6$, $F(1, 151) = 16.03$, $p < .001$. As women were more likely to describe themselves as having feminine characteristics they were more likely to embrace an image of God with feminine characteristics.

The third hypothesis predicted that there would be a positive relationship between participants' gender role identities and the gender related characteristics they attribute to God. Three sets of product moment correlations were conducted to test this hypothesis. Correlation coefficients were computed for men and women combined, men alone and women alone across the three scales for gender role identity (masculine gender role identity, feminine gender role identity, and the attitudes toward women scale) and the two scales for gender role characteristics attributed to God (images of God with feminine characteristic and images of God with masculine characteristics). The alpha level was set at .001 to help control for Type I error. Feminine images of God were positively related to participants' feminine gender role identity for the entire sample ($r = .42$) and for men alone ($r = .47$) and for women alone ($r = .31$). Similarly, masculine images of God were negatively related to nontraditional attitudes toward women for everyone ($r = -.21$), for men alone

($r = -.28$), and for women alone ($r = -.26$). Table 1 presents the complete correlations.

The last hypothesis predicted that men and women would differ in their perceptions of God as male, female, masculine and feminine. Since these four outcome measures were significantly correlated, a one-way multivariate analysis of variance (MANOVA) was conducted. Significant differences were found between men and women, Hotelling's Trace $= .031$, $F (4, 267) = 2.55$, $p = .039$. Discriminant analyses indicated that feminine images of God was the most powerful discriminator (Standardized discriminant function coefficient $= 1.00$). This finding was confirmed by follow-up analyses of variance. Men and women were significantly different on perceptions of God having feminine characteristics, $F (1, 270) = 8.13$, $p = .005$. Women are more likely than men to view God as having feminine characteristics. Table 2 contains the means and standard deviations on the dependent variables across sexes.

Post Hoc Analyses

In the Catholic Church, God is typically referred to as Father; therefore, whether participants' gender role attitudes would predict endorse-

TABLE 1. Correlations Between Scales of Gender Role Identity and God's Gender Related Characteristics for Men and Women Combined

	God Masculine	God Feminine
All participants:		
Bem masculine	.07	.13
Bem feminine	.16	.42*
Attitude toward women	−.21*	−.04
Men only:		
Bem masculine	.11	.21
Bem feminine	.13	.47*
Attitude toward women	−.28*	−.09
Women only:		
Bem masculine	−.01	.09
Bem feminine	.13	.31*
Attitude toward women	−.26*	−.02

*$p \leq .001$

TABLE 2. Means and Standard Deviations on the Dependent Variables for Both Genders

| | Men | | Women | |
Image of God	M	SD	M	SD
God as male	9.08	2.04	9.10	1.98
God as female	6.01	3.10	7.07	3.08
God as masculine	3.26	.41	3.29	.37
God as feminine	3.66	.35	3.77	.29

ment of the item, Father, was examined. Feminine gender role identity and attitudes toward women were entered as a cluster and together were significant predictors, $R^2 = 6.4$ percent, $F (3, 278) = 6.32$, $p = < .001$. When the correlations between endorsement of father and attitudes toward women and feminine gender role identity were examined, only the correlation between father and nontraditional attitudes toward women was significant, $r = -.21$, $p = .001$.

DISCUSSION

According to the findings, images of God as female (mother, sister, woman) were predicted from feminine gender role identity and nontraditional attitudes toward women. The greater a person's feminine gender role identity and the more nontraditional his or her attitude toward women, the more likely he or she was to endorse images of God as female. Masculine gender role identity was not predictive of images of God as female. Furthermore, the results indicated that images of God as male (father, brother, man) could also be predicted from feminine gender role identity and attitudes toward women. The higher one's feminine gender role identity and the more traditional his or her attitude toward women, the more likely he or she was to endorse images of God as male.

While these results may seem ambiguous, clarity is gained when the predictors are examined individually. Attitudes toward women is fairly straightforward, indicating that more traditional attitudes toward women (e.g., agreement with statements "A woman's place is in the home looking after her family, rather than following a career of her own" or "It sounds worse when a woman swears than when a man does") are associated with images of God as male and less traditional attitudes toward women (e.g., agreement with statements such as, "Women earning as much as their dates should pay for themselves when going out with them" or "If a woman goes out to work her husband should share the housework, such as washing dishes, cleaning and cooking") are associated with images of God as female. However, feminine gender identity (perception of self as affectionate, sympathetic, sensitive to needs of others, understanding, compassionate, eager to soothe hurt feelings, warm, tender, love children, and gentle) as a predictor for both images of God as male (father, brother, man) and images of God as female (mother, sister, woman) is less clear, especially given that masculine gender role identity (perception of self as independent, assertive, aggressive, forceful, willing to take risks, dominant, willing to take a stand and defend beliefs and having a strong personality) was not significantly correlated with either images of God as male or images of God as female. Perhaps men and women with strong feminine gender identity are more relationship oriented and, therefore, more likely to endorse both male and female anthropomorphized images of God.

Like the predictors of images of God as male and female, the predictors for images of God with feminine and masculine characteristics were also complex. Feminine gender role identity was the primary independent variable that predicted images of God with feminine characteristics (beautiful, comforting, compassionate, gentle, giving, life-giver, listener, loving, nature, nice, peaceful, precious, pure, spiritual and welcoming) for both men and women. While this supports projection theory, that men and women see God as they see themselves, it does not uniformly support the hypothesis that nontraditional gender role identity is positively related to images of God with feminine characteristics. Full support of that hypothesis would require a positive correlation between masculine (non-traditional) gender identity for women and an image of God with feminine characteristics. Such a relationship was not found.

Furthermore, results indicated that for men there was a significant correlation between masculine (traditional) gender role identity and images of God with feminine characteristics. Although this finding may raise doubt as to the relevance of a positive correlation between feminine (non-traditional) gender role identity and images of God with feminine characteristics for men, one finding does not impact the other. The masculine and feminine scales of gender role identity are independent, indicating that an individual can have both feminine and masculine characteristics (Constantinople, 1973); therefore, men with high masculine gender role identity may still be considered non-traditional if they also identify themselves as having feminine characteristics associated with feminine gender role identity.

Attitudes toward women was not significantly related to images of God with feminine characteristics for either men or women. However, traditional attitudes toward women was the only independent variable that predicted images of God with masculine characteristics (active, all-knowing, controls our fate, creator, guide, intimidating, judge, lawmaker, life-taker, logical, Messiah, powerful, protector, punishing, relentless, strong, superior, unafraid, wise). Neither feminine nor masculine gender role identity were predictors of images of God with masculine characteristics. This finding does not support projection theory, that people see God as they see themselves. However, it does support the assertions that people with more traditional attitudes toward women are more likely to see God as masculine, just as they are more likely to see God as male.

Sex of the participants was found to be a moderating variable for images of God with masculine and feminine characteristics. Women were more likely to attribute God with feminine characteristics than men were. However, the small proportion of variance accounted for by sex indicated that gender role identity, rather than sex, was a more significant predictor of feminine images of God.

Consequently, all analyses indicate that feminine gender identity is a significant predictor of feminine images of God, as well as images of God as male and as female. Attitudes toward women is a predictor of male images of God as well as images of God with masculine characteristics. In support of the literature reviewed, this study demonstrated the dynamic interplay of gender identity and attitudes toward women as they relate to images of God. According to previous image of God research based on projection theory, people often see God as they see themselves. Feminist theologians, however, argue that images of God are inextricably bound to gender role socialization. People who ascribe to a patriarchal social system will embrace male images of God that support that system. Consequently, these two theories may predict seemingly conflictual images of God, especially for people who have a high feminine gender role identity and endorse a social system that perpetuates male privilege.

According to the findings, people with more traditional attitudes toward women will be more likely to see God as male (father, brother, man) than as female (mother, sister, woman) and more likely to see God with masculine characteristics (active, all-knowing, controls our fate, creator, guide, intimidating, judge, lawmaker, life-taker, logical, Messiah, powerful, protector, punishing, relentless, strong, superior, unafraid, wise) rather than God with feminine characteristics (beautiful, comforting, compassionate, gentle, giving, life-giver, listener, loving, nature, nice, peaceful, precious, pure, spiritual, welcoming). Furthermore, the findings indicate that people with strong feminine gender identity are more likely to have both male and female images of God and to view God as having feminine characteristics. Consequently, it seems that an individual who has both traditional attitudes toward women, as well as feminine gender identity, would probably experience some cognitive dissonance, due to the interweaving of socialization and projection associated with God images. On the one hand, the person may perceive God as having feminine characteristics like him or herself. On the other hand, the person may view God as having masculine characteristics consistent with patriarchal models of power. Since this study did not require participants to choose between masculine and feminine characteristics for God, it is possible that such a person would have an image of God with both masculine and feminine characteristics. This image of God would represent the dynamic interplay between projection theory, in which the person with feminine gender identity sees God as having feminine characteristics like him or herself, and feminist theological theories, in which the person with traditional attitudes toward women is more likely to endorse images of God as male and masculine.

Although the authors of this paper are not scholars of theology or religious studies, as lay women, we recognize that the Bible (International Bible Society,1984) repeatedly endorses traditional attitudes toward women that promote the dominant role of men and the submissive role of women. For example, in Ephesians (5:22, 5:24, and 5:33, NIV), Colossians (3:18, NIV), Titus (2:5, NIV) and 1 Peter (3:1 and 3:5, NIV), women are instructed to be submissive to their husbands. Husbands must be considerate in return and "treat them with respect as the weaker partner" (1 Peter 3:7, NIV).

Likewise, it seems that male and masculine images of God, advanced by the Hebrew Bible long before the birth of Jesus, have also dominated Christian social systems. In the New Testament God is referred to as Father (Matthew 23:8-10, NIV), King (Matthew 25:33-41, NIV), Judge (James 4:11-13, NIV), Ruler (1 Timothy 6:15, NIV), and Master (Colossians 4:1-2, NIV), associated with attributes of justice, power, retribution, and punishment. These images vividly typify God as male with masculine gender role characteristics.

This study supports the assertion that people who embrace traditional attitudes toward women are more likely to embrace images of God as male and masculine. This correlation is possibly a consequence of the common historical and scriptural foundation of both the independent and dependent variable. In addition to scripture, religious tradition and doctrine further perpetuate both traditional attitudes toward women and images of God as male. The absence of inclusive language in the Catholic Church is a contemporary example of how traditional attitudes toward women and images of God as male continue to be sustained.

Horizontal inclusive language is the use of gender neutral terms when talking about human beings, while vertical inclusive language is the use of gender neutral terms when discussing God. While the U.S. Catholic Bishops have never approved of vertical inclusive language for church texts, throughout the 1990s they have debated the use of horizontal inclusive language used in the lectionary, and thus in Catholic Mass (Allen, 1998). In 1997, after six years of discussion, a working group of 11 men (four archbishops, five advisers and two note-takers) were appointed by the Holy See to determine the extent to which inclusive language could be used in the U.S. lectionary. While these men permitted changes in the term adelphoi to be translated as "brothers and sisters," as opposed to "brothers," they did not permit changes of the word "man" into the word "person" or the word "his" to the plural "their."

Although God continues to be characterized as male in the Catholic Church, many Catholics in the United States ascribe feminine characteristics to God, especially in recent years. This is supported by Hertel and Donahue (1995) and Nelson et al. (1985) who found that supportive images of God were more prevalent than authoritarian images of God.

The results of this study demonstrate how seemingly conflictual theories of projection and gender role socialization can complementarily explain gender related images of God. The explanatory powers of these theories are limited, however, and the modest results of this study are weakened by low internal reliability for the image of God as male scale. Furthermore, the gender role identity and attitudes of participants in this study were not compared to data on gender role identity and attitudes in the general population. Consequently, it is unknown as to whether study participants had more or less masculine or feminine characteristics or traditional attitudes toward women than the general population. According to Thompson's (1991) assertion, men and women who are religiously active are more likely to have a feminine orientation.

In addition, this study did not analyze the prevalence of male and female images of God or the prevalence of images of God with masculine and feminine characteristics. While these analyses were not directly related to the hypotheses of the study, they would have provided interesting information to compare with previous findings. In particular, it would have been valuable to assess if these findings support Roof and Roof's (1984) findings that male images of God are more abundant than female images of God for Americans, Vergote et al.'s (1969) assertion that the primary image of God is paternal, or Kunkel et al.'s (1999) finding that traditional male images (father God) were more salient than female God images (mother God) for college students, even though they embraced images of God with feminine gender role characteristics.

Furthermore, this study only surveyed students attending mass at Catholic student communities associated with universities in the Southwest. It is possible that Catholic churches in the Southwest support images of God and gender role attitudes that differ from churches in other regions in the country. It is also possible that church-attending Catholic students vary greatly from Catholic students who do not attend church. Finally, university-enrolled Catholics may not be representative of the general Catholic population in the United States; therefore, it is important that the findings of this study are not generalized beyond the participants represented. Additionally, it would be interesting to compare Catholics with people from other Christian religions, as well as people from non-Christian religions.

This study is one of only a few quantitative examinations of images of God and gender role identity and attitudes. From these findings it is evident that perceptions of God are related to gender attitudes. These initial results need to be replicated and extended in future research.

REFERENCES

Allen, John L. 1998, September 25. On the lectionary, 11 men made the deal. *National Catholic Reporter*, p. A1.

Baker, Douglas D. & Terpstra, David E. 1986. Locus of control and self-esteem versus demographic factors as predictors of attitudes toward women. *Basic and Applied Social Psychology*, 7(2), 163-172.

Bem, Sandra. 1974. The measurement of psychological androgyny. *Journal of Consulting and Clinical Psychology*, 42, (2), 155-162.

Bem, Sandra. 1981. *Bem Sex-Role Inventory Manual*, Redwood City, CA: Mind Garden.

Benson, Peter L., & Spilka, Bernard. 1973. God image as a function of self-esteem and locus of control. *Journal for the Scientific Study of Religion*, 12, 297-30.

Campbell, Todd, & Arthur, James. 1997. BEM sex-role inventory: Educational tests and measurements. *Educational & Psychological Measurement*, 57(1), 118-125.

Constantinople, Anne. 1973. Masculinity-Femininity: An exception to a famous dictum? *Psychological Bulletin*, 80(5), 389-407.

Durkheim, Emile 1972. The social foundations of religion. In R. Robertson (Ed.), *Sociology of Religion* (pp. 42-53). Baltimore, MD: Penguin Books Inc. (Original work published 1912).

Etaugh, Claire, & Spandikow, Deborah Bohn. 1981. Changing attitudes toward women: A longitudinal study of college students. *Psychology of Women Quarterly*, 5(4), 591-594.

Feuerbach, Ludwig. 1957. *The essence of Christianity*. (E. G. Waring & F. W. Strothmann, Eds.). New York: Frederick Ungar Publishing. (Original work published 1841).

Foster, R. A., & Keating, J. P. 1992. Research note measuring androcentrism in the Western God-concept. *Journal for the Scientific Study of Religion*, 31(3), 366-375.

Hertel, Bradley & Donahue, Michael. 1995. Parental influences on God images among children: Testing Durkheim's metaphoric parallelism. *Journal for the Scientific Study of Religion*, 34(2), 186-200.

International Bible Society. 1984. *Holy Bible, new international version*. Grand Rapids, MI: Zondervon Publishing House.

Johnson, Elizabeth. 1992. *She who is: The mystery of God in feminist theological discourse*. New York: The Crossroad Publishing Company.

Kunkel, Mark, Cook, Stephen, Meshel, David, Daughtry, Donald, & Hauenstein, Anita. 1999. Image of God; God images: A concept map. *Journal for the Scientific Study of Religion*, 38(2), 193-203.

Nelsen, Hart M., Cheek, Neil, H., & Au, Paul. 1985. Gender differences in images of God. *Journal for the Scientific Study of Religion*, 24(4), 396-402.

Nelson, M.C., 1988. Reliability, validity, and cross-cultural comparisons for the simplified Attitudes Toward Women Scale. *Sex Roles*, 18 (5/6), 289-296.

Rhodes, A. Lewis. 1983. Effects of religious denominations on sex differences in occupational expectations. *Sex Roles*, 9(1), 93-108.

Roberts, Carl W. 1989. Imagining God: Who is created in whose image? *Review of Religious Research* 30(4), 375-386.

Roof, Wade Clark, & Roof, Jennifer L. 1984. Review of the polls: Images of God Among Americans. *Journal for the Scientific Study of Religion*, 23(2), 201-205.

Schoenfeld, Eugen, & Mestrovic, Stjepan. 1991. With justice and mercy: Instrumental-masculine and expressive-feminine elements in religion. *Journal for the Scientific Study of Religion*, 30(4), 363-380.

Spence, Janet T., Helmreich, Robert, & Stapp, Joy. 1975. Ratings of self and peers on sex role attributes and their relation to self-esteem and conceptions of masculinity and femininity. *Journal of Personality and Social Psychology*, 32(1), 29-39.

Thompson, Edward H. 1991. Beneath the status characteristic: Gender variations in religiousness. *Journal for the Scientific Study of Religion*, 30(4), 381-394.

Vergote, Antoine, Tamayo, Alvaro, Pasquali, Luiz, Bonami, Michel, Pattyn, Ma-
rie-Rose, & Custers, Anne. 1969. Concept of God and parental images. *Journal for
the Scientific Study of Religion* 8, 79-87.

Vergote, Antoine, & Tamayo, Alvaro. (1981). *The parental figures and the representation of god: A psychological and cross-cultural study.* The Hague: Mouton Press.

Reflections on a Study
in a Mental Hospital

Richard Dayringer, ThD

SUMMARY. A Chaplain conducted semi-structured interviews using religious questions with 77 patients at the East Louisiana State Hospital. Findings included 78 percent who agreed with the teachings of their church, 64 percent were church members, 63 percent had experienced a religious conversion, 58 percent reported having guilt feelings, 51 percent regularly practiced prayer, 33 percent thought it was God's will for them to be in the hospital, 29 percent reported regular church attendance, 26 percent concluded that their faith helped them to cope with their illness and hospitalization, and 22 percent said that they had either seen God or heard Him speak. *[Article copies available for a fee from The Haworth Document Delivery Service: 1-800-HAWORTH. E-mail address: <docdelivery@haworthpress.com> Website: <http://www.HaworthPress.com> © 2004 by The Haworth Press, Inc. All rights reserved.]*

Dr. Richard Dayringer is Editor of the *American Journal of Pastoral Counseling*; Adjunct Professor, University of Oklahoma College of Medicine-Tulsa; and Professor Emeritus, Southern Illinois University School of Medicine.

An earlier version of this paper appeared online at the Wayne E. Oates Institute, Fall Conference, October 1999.

[Haworth co-indexing entry note]: "Reflections on a Study in a Mental Hospital." Dayringer, Richard. Co-published simultaneously in *American Journal of Pastoral Counseling* (The Haworth Pastoral Press, an imprint of The Haworth Press, Inc.) Vol. 7, No. 2, 2004, pp. 77-89; and: *The Image of God and the Psychology of Religion* (ed: Richard Dayringer, and David Oler) The Haworth Pastoral Press, an imprint of The Haworth Press, Inc., 2004, pp. 77-89. Single or multiple copies of this article are available for a fee from The Haworth Document Delivery Service [1-800-HAWORTH, 9:00 a.m. - 5:00 p.m. (EST). E-mail address: docdelivery@haworthpress.com].

KEYWORDS. Belief, Bible, church, conversion faith, God's will, guilt, prayer, religion

While doing doctoral studies at the New Orleans Baptist Theological Seminary (NOBTS), I was given a 12 month study grant by the Department of Mental Health in the state of Louisiana to do research and ministry at the East Louisiana State Hospital (ELSH) in Jackson. I also participated with the four first year psychiatric residents from Tulane University School of Medicine in their educational and clinical activities.

For my research project, I chose to do a semi-structured religious interview with patients, most of whom were newly admitted. For many years, religion or spirituality was considered by some mental health professionals to be a strong contributor to mental illness (Freud [1927], 1962; Ellis, 1980; Watters, 1992). Any positive role that religion played in the treatment of mental illness received little attention. Actually, researchers (<biblio>) largely ignored the relationship between religion and mental illness. When religion was included, it was often measured in cursory fashion and the results were not always discussed (Larson et al., 1986; Levin, 1994).

As a religious professional, I naturally hypothesized (and hoped) that mental patients found religion to be helpful during their hospitalization, and not a contributing factor to their illness. Historically, mental health professionals have viewed beliefs in the power of God and prayer as "magical thinking." They tried to avoid discussions of the "unholy trinity" which included religion, finances, and politics.

REVIEW OF THE LITERATURE

Recent Gallup surveys report that 95 percent of Americans believe in God, 90 percent pray, and 43 percent attend religious services at least weekly (Princeton Religion Research Center, 1996). Eighty-seven percent of persons answering a recent NEWSWEEK survey said they believed that God answers prayers (The Mystery of Prayer, 1997). Eighty-two percent of respondents to a CNN/TIME poll said that they believed in the healing power of prayer (Faith and Healing, 1996).

Kroll and Sheehan (1989) studied the religious beliefs, practices, and experiences of 52 patients (19 men and 33 women) admitted to a psychiatric hospital in Minnesota. Thirty-one percent had a diagnosis of major depression, 21 percent manic episode, 19 percent schizophrenia, 19 percent personality disorder, and 8 percent anxiety disorder. Ninety-five percent believed in God; 55 percent of women and 47 percent of men attended church weekly and prayed and read their Bibles. Sixty-eight percent of men and 33 percent of women reported having had a personal religious experience. The authors also concluded that religion played only a small role in arousing the guilt that underlies depression.

Lindgren and Coursey (1995) interviewed 30 psychiatric patients in Maryland. Diagnoses included schizophrenia (67 percent), bipolar disorder (10 percent), unipolar disorder (7 percent), schizoaffective disorder (3 percent), personality disorder (3 percent), and other (10 percent). Fifty-seven percent of the patients attended religious services and also reported praying daily. Eighty-three percent felt that their spiritual belief had a positive impact on their illness because of the comfort it provided.

At a Chicago medical center, Fitchett, Burton, and Sivan (1997) surveyed and compared the religious beliefs of 51 adult psychiatric patients with 50 general medical patients matched for age and gender. Diagnoses for the psychiatric patients were as follows: major depression (39 percent), bipolar depression (28 percent), schizoaffective disorder (14 percent), and other (20 percent). Concerning the psychiatric patients, 80 percent considered themselves to be religious persons and 48 percent indicated that they were "deeply religious." Sixty-eight percent said they relied on their religion as a source of strength "a great deal" and only 10 percent reported "none" or "not at all." Thirty-four percent attended religious services once weekly or more. In regard to spiritual needs, 84 percent needed to know of God's presence, 80 percent needed prayer, and 65 percent needed a visit from the chaplain.

Delusions with religious content are not rare in psychotic disorders and may be present in as many as 10 to 15 percent of hospitalized patients diagnosed as schizophrenic (Koenig and Weaver, 1997). These delusions, however, are most likely a manifestation of the psychotic illness rather than the cause for it (cf. Wilson's chapter in Koenig, 1998). Conversion experiences were found to be more likely to occur in patients with affective disorders because of their greater capacity for affective expression (Gallemore, Wilson, and Rhoads, 1969).

Propst and colleagues (1992) examined the effectiveness of using religion-based psychotherapy in the treatment of 59 depressed religious patients. This religious therapy used Christian religious rationales, religious arguments to counter irrational thoughts, and religious imagery. Religious therapy resulted in significantly faster recovery from depression when compared with standard secular cognitive-behavioral therapy. An astonishing finding was that clinical benefits from religious-based therapy were most evident among patients who received religious therapy from *nonreligious* therapists.

Chu and Klein (1985), after studying 128 African-Americans diagnosed with schizophrenia, concluded that these patients were less likely to be rehospitalized if their families encouraged them to continue religious worship while they were in the hospital.

The two studies with which I was most familiar when I did my research were both published in the fifties. Oates (1955) interviewed 68 patients at the Kentucky State Hospital at Danville in about 1950. He concluded that 17 percent revealed a conflict of either long-standing rebellion or submission toward the religion of his or her home. Ten percent clutched at religion as a "last straw" attempt to solve unmanageable problems. Twenty percent had psychotic conditions, which were simply "clothed" in religious ideas. Fifty-two percent showed no evidence of religious interest or past religious influence.

Southard (1956) studied 173 first admission patients from 1951 to 1953 at Central State Hospital in Lakeland, KY. Fourteen percent of the patients used religion to supply the words and phrases by which they talked about their problems. In half of these patients, their religious ideas receded as the patient became quieter. The other half had a fixed delusional system. Twelve percent of the patients derived very positive benefits from their religion. Five percent raised issues which involved direct violation of community moral standards. Sixty-six percent had no particular religious interests.

Combined observations of these two studies indicate that (1) religious affiliation with this or that group had little or no correlation with mental illness, (2) the church had little if any influence either way on half of hospitalized mental patients, (3) the way religious teachings were presented to a person had much to do with the way he or she accepted, rejected or fell into interminable conflict over religion, and (4) the concept of God and the concept of parents may have developed obstructive "adhesions" to each other in the religious perception of the patient.

METHODOLOGY

The methodology used in this research was simple and straightforward. I interviewed patients (one-on-one) on the respective female and male admitting wards soon after their admission. I also interviewed patients in the Security Treatment Area (STA) of the hospital who had been legally committed as criminally insane. After establishing rapport, I obtained information concerning the following questions in a semi-structured manner.

1. What is your religion or denominational preference?
2. Are you a member of a religious group?
3. Have you experienced a religious conversion or confirmation?
4. Do you agree with the beliefs of your denomination?
5. Have you usually attended religious services regularly?
6. Do you pray?
7. Do you read the Bible?
8. Do you feel that it was God's will that you be hospitalized?
9. Has your religion/faith been helpful during your illness?
10. Have you seen God or heard God speak?
11. Do you feel guilty?

Notes were written during or immediately after these interviews. Findings were analyzed and calculated into percentages or averages.

FINDINGS

Altogether 77 patients were interviewed. One refused to talk to me leaving 76 interviews to be analyzed: 34 females and 43 males. Seventy-three were Caucasian and three were African-American. The age range was 16 to 75 with an average age of 42: 38 for females and 46 for males.

Diagnoses for the patients interviewed were as follows: paranoid schizophrenic 18, schizophrenic 13, schizophrenic and depressed 8, brain syndrome 8, depressed 7, sociopath 3, and one each of dissociated personality, retarded, and schizoid personality. The diagnosis for 16 patients was unknown or unrecorded.

Sixty-seven preferred a Christian denomination including: Baptist 39, Methodist 9, Roman Catholic 7, Church of Christ 3, Episcopal 3, Lutheran 2, and one each of Christian, Christian Science, Greek Orthodox, and Unitarian; 1 was an atheist. Forty-nine were church members including: Baptist 28, Roman Catholic 7, Methodist 5, Episcopal 3, Church of Christ 2, Lutheran 2, and one each of Greek Orthodox and Unitarian. Thirty-six reported having experienced a religious conversion and 12 had been confirmed. This is a combined total of 48 or 63 percent.

Thirty-eight ((78 percent) said that they agreed with the beliefs or teachings of their church. Others pled ignorance, naivete, disinterest, confusion, or disagreement in regard to these beliefs.

Twenty-two patients (29 percent) reported regular attendance at religious services. Fifteen said they had been regular in attendance during at least one period of their lives. Thirty-one stated that they had never been regular in attending church services.

The practice of prayer was reported by the majority of the patients: 39 (51 percent) affirmed it. Six said that they read their Bibles frequently. Twelve said that they did not pray and others gave no answer.

Of those who responded, 25 (33 percent) thought it was God's will for them to be in the hospital and 28 did not believe it was God's will for them to be there. Two thought, rather, that it was the devil that had put them in the hospital.

Nineteen or 26 percent concluded that their faith had helped them to cope with their illness and hospitalization. Nine patients spoke of God's love in response to this question, but two said they were not sure God loved them; and eight spoke of various kinds of fear. Four indicated that their faith helped their self-esteem. Four spoke of God's forgiveness, but one could not feel God's forgiveness. Two spoke of God's mercy but two others spoke of God's vengefulness. Two talked about God's mercy but one said that God was unfair. Five preferred not to discuss this subject.

The great majority of the patients interviewed stated that they had never seen nor heard God. However, nine said that they had heard God speak and eight reported that they had seen God (a combined percentage of 22). Three of them described him as being an elderly bewhiskered man. One person said that she had seen the Virgin Mary.

Forty-four patients (58 percent) reported guilty feelings and 23 named specific behaviors about which they felt guilty. Sixteen said they had never experienced guilt.

Table 1 which follows present the findings of this research in summary fashion. The figures are given in totals or percentages.

DISCUSSION

I chose this topic of research with some thought given to making it my doctoral dissertation but ultimately selected a different subject

TABLE 1

	A	B	C	D	E	F	G	H	I
	AGE	GENDER	RACE	DIAGNOSIS	REL. PREF.	MEMBER	CONV. CONF.	DENOM. BELIEFS	ATTENDANCE
1									
2	16 to 75	F: 33	Caucasion: 73	Par. Schiz.: 18	Baptist: 39	Baptist: 28	Converted: 36	Yes: 37	Yes: 22
3	Averages: 42	M: 43	Af.-Am: 3	Schiz: 13	Methodist: 9	Methodist: 9	Confirmed: 12		Formerly: 15
4	F: 38			Schiz & Dep: 8	Rom. Cath.: 7	Rom. Cath.: 7			No: 31
5	M: 46			Brain Syn: 8	Ch. of Christ: 3	Ch. of Christ: 2			
6				Dep: 7	Episcopal: 3	Episcopal: 3			
7				Sociopath: 3	Lutheran: 2	Lutheran: 2			
8				Dissociated: 1	Christian: 1				
9				Retarded: 1	Chris. Sc.: 1				
10				Schizoid: 1	Greek Cath.: 1	Greek Cath.: 1			
11					Unitarian: 1	Unitarian: 1			
12					Atheist: 1				
13	TOTALS:	76	76	60	67	53	48		29
14	PERCENTAGES:					0.64	0.63	0.7	0.29

TABLE 1 (continued)

	J	K	L	M	N	O	P
1	PRAY	READ BIBLE	GOD'S WILL	FAITH HELPFUL	SEE/HEAR GOD	GUILTY	
2	Yes: 39	Yes: 6	Yes: 25	Yes: 19	Heard: 9	Yes: 44	
3	No: 12		No: 28	No:16	Saw: 8	No: 16	
4					No: 46	Gave reason: 23	
5							
6							
7							
8							
9							
10							
11							
12							
13							
14	0.51	0.08	0.33	0.26	0.22	0.58	

(Dayringer, 1998). At the time I decided that my total number of subjects was too small to be of significance. Now, in surveying the literature to write this paper, I realize that the size of my study is comparable to many of those cited above (e.g., Kroll and Sheehan, 1989; Lindgren and Coursey, 1995; Fitchett, Burton, and Sivan, 1997; and Oates, 1955). One of the main things that appealed to me about this research was that it incorporated ministry into the work that I was assigned to do at the hospital.

As a group, the patients whom I interviewed for this study were most interesting. The interviews usually took place within a few days of their arrival at the hospital except for those at the STA. With the exception of one patient who was interviewed on her twenty-first day and one on her seventeenth, the remainder was interviewed from one to 12 calendar days after admission.

The great predominance of Baptists in this study does not indicate that more Baptists become mentally ill than people in other religious groups. The denominational preferences represent the population of the hospital catchment area at that time.

The fact that only three African-Americans appear in this study is simply the result of my hospital assignment during the period of the study. However, African-American patients (then and there called "Negroes" or "blacks") were at that time in Louisiana housed in separate buildings, and separate restrooms and water fountains for them were so designated. In fact, I was once seriously reprimanded for addressing African-American males as "sir."

Sixty-four percent of the patients in this study were church members. This, of course, means that 46 percent were not affiliated with a church. Oates (1955) found that 52 percent of his subjects were not church members and 66 percent of Southard's (1956) patients were unaffiliated religiously. Thus, all these studies indicate that only about half of all hospitalized mental patients are church members.

If Kroll and Sheehan's (1989) figures for males and females are combined, 56 percent of his subjects reported a religious experience. Sixty-three percent of the patients I interviewed reported conversion or confirmation. Thus, the patients in my study appear to have been slightly more religiously oriented or committed than the other studies mentioned in this paragraph.

Thirty-seven patients (70 percent) in the present research stated that they agreed with the religious beliefs of their denomination. No comparable category exists in the other studies referenced.

Regular church attendance was reported by 29 percent of the ELSH sample. Forty-three percent of Americans generally attend worship services (Princeton Religion Research Center, 1996). Kroll and Sheehan (1989) reported that 55 percent of women and 47 percent of men in their study attended church weekly. Fifty-seven percent of Lindgren and Coursey's (1995) patients attended religious services and 34 percent of Fitchett, Burton, and Sivan's (1997) mental patients attended religious services once weekly or more. If those in the ELSH study who formerly attended worship regularly are combined with those who did at the time, then 49 percent of the ELSH sample compares nicely with the average of all these studies: 47 percent.

Prayer was reported by 51 percent of the ELSH sample. Ninety percent of Americans pray (Princeton Religion Research Center, 1996). In the Kroll and Sheehan (1989) study, 55 percent of women and 47 percent of men prayed. Lindgren and Coursey (1995) reported that 57 percent of their sample prayed daily. Thus, findings concerning prayer in this study compare quite favorably with other research.

Only eight percent of ELSH patients reported Bible reading. Kroll and Sheehan (1989) reported that 55 percent of women and 47 percent of men read their Bibles. I cannot account easily for the large difference in these findings.

Twenty-five or 33 percent of the ELSH patients felt that it was God's will for them to be hospitalized. This factor was not measured in the other studies cited herein.

Twenty-six percent of the patients in this study reported that their faith had been helpful during their illness and or hospitalization. Eighty-three percent of Lindgren and Coursey's (1995) patients, 68 percent of the mental patients in the Fitchett, Burton, and Sivan (1997) study, and 12 percent of Southard's (1956) patients reported that their faith or beliefs had been helpful. The range of findings in this area from 12 to 83 percent is wide indeed. The average of these figures is 47 percent. If those who found their faith to be helpful are divided only by the Christian church members in the ELSH study, the figure is 41 percent. This means that my hypothesis was not correct. Less than half of the patients in this study reported that their religion was helpful during times of mental illness.

Koenig and Weaver (1997) reported that as many as 10 to 15 percent of hospitalized patients diagnosed as schizophrenic report delusions with religious content. Delusions were not measured among patients in the present study. Auditory and visual hallucinations having religious content were recorded. Twenty-two percent had experiences of hearing (12 percent) or seeing (11 percent [these percentages are rounded])

God. Therefore, almost half of the patients in the present study could be said to have an image of God as knowing their situation, caring, forgiving, guiding, and hearing their prayers.

Fifty-eight percent of the ELSH sample of patients reported having guilt feelings. Only Kroll and Sheehan (1989) mention (without giving any figures) guilt feelings in the studies that I have cited.

The 17 patients that I interviewed on the STA had all been hospitalized from one to several years. Almost all of them had murdered one or more people. The guards cautioned me to be very careful with three of them especially and wondered why they were on the list to be seen by me. Nevertheless, they were all cooperative and responsive.

In addition to whatever ministry of pastoral care seemed to be appropriate to incorporate during these interviews, I often made follow-up visits as well. A few of these patients were referred to me for pastoral counseling. I also was conducting an extended unit of Clinical Pastoral Education with five doctoral students from NOBTS at the time and often referred certain patients to them for follow-up pastoral care and counseling.

CONCLUSION

- Approximately half of hospitalized mental patients are church members.
- More than half of hospitalized mental patients have experienced a religious conversion or confirmation of their faith.
- Seventy-eight percent of the mental patients in the ELSH study agreed with the beliefs of their respective denominations.
- Roughly one-third to one-half of hospitalized mental patients usually attend religious services regularly.
- About half of hospitalized mental patients pray.
- The range of hospitalized mental patients who read their Bibles is from eight to 55 percent.
- One-third of the mental patients in the ELSH study felt that it was God's will for them to be in the hospital.

By averaging the wide range of 12 to 83 percent reported in four studies, one could say that approximately half of hospitalized mental patients reported that their faith had been helpful to them during the time of their illness and hospitalization.

Ten to 15 percent of hospitalized patients reported delusions with religious content in one study. In the ELSH study, 22 percent of patients said they had seen God or heard him speak.

Slightly more than half of the ELSH patients reported that they had felt guilty.

I have, until now, left the question of when the present study was done purposefully unanswered in an effort to maintain the reader's interest. The interviews reported in this research were done in 1964. I had never found the time or motivation to analyze this data until now.

REFERENCES

Chu, C.C. and Klein, H.E. (1985). "Psychosocial and Environmental Variables in Outcome of Black Schizophrenics." *Journal of the National Medical Association,* 77:793-796.

Dayringer, R. ([1989] 1998). *The Heart of Pastoral Counseling,* Second edition. Binghamton, NY: Haworth.

Ellis, A. (1980). "Psychotherapy and Atheistic Values: A Response to AE Bergin's 'Psychotherapy and Religious Values'." *Journal of Consulting and Clinical Psychology,* 48:642-645.

"Faith and Healing: Can Prayer, Faith and Spirituality Really Improve Your Physical Health?" *Time,* June 24, 1996, pp. 58-68.

Fitchett, G., Burton, L.A., and Sivan, A.B. (1997). "The Religious Needs and Resources of Psychiatric Patients." *Journal of Nervous and Mental Disease,* 185:320-326.

Freud, S. ([1927] 1962). *The Future of an Illusion.* London: Hogarth.

Gallemore, J.A.L., Wilson, W.P., and Rhoads, J.A.M. (1969). "The Religious Life of Patients with Affective Disorders." *Diseases of the Nervous System,* 30:483-486.

Koenig, H.J. and Weaver, A.J. (1997). *Counseling Troubled Older Adults: A Handbook for Pastors and Religious Caregivers.* Nashville: Abingdon.

Kroll, J. and Sheehan, W. (1989). "Religious Beliefs and Practices among 52 Psychiatric Inpatients in Minnesota." *American Journal of Psychiatry,* 146:67-72.

Larson, D.C. and Milano, M.A.G. (1997). "Making the Case for Spiritual Interventions in Clinical Practice." *Mind/Body Medicine,* 2(1):20-30.

Larson, D.C., Pattison, E.M., Blazer, D.C., Omran, A.R., and Kaplan, B.A.H. (1986). "Systematic Analysis of Research on Religious Variables in Four Major Psychiatric Journals, 1978-1982." *American Journal of Psychiatry,* 143:329-334.

Lindgren, K.N. and Coursey, R.D. (1995). "Spirituality and Serious Mental Illness: A Two-part Study." *Psychosocial Rehabilitation Journal,* 18(3): 93-111.

"The Mystery of Prayer: Does God Play Favorites?" *Newsweek,* Mar. 31, 1997, pp. 56-65.

Princeton Religion Research Center. (1996). *Religion in America*. Princeton, NJ: The Gallup Poll.

Propst, L.R., Ostrom, R., Watkins, P., Dean, T., and Mashburn, D. (1992). "Comparative Efficacy of Religious and Nonreligious Cognitive-behavior Therapy for the Treatment of Clinical Depression in Religious Individuals." *Journal of Consulting and Clinical Psychology*, 60:94-103.

Watters, W.W. (1992). *Deadly Doctrine*. New York: Prometheus.

The Formation of Adolescents' Image of God: Predictors and Age and Gender Differences

Augustine Meier
Molisa Meier

SUMMARY. The goal of this research was to assess age and gender differences on adolescents' image of God using standardized instruments and to assess variables for their power to predict God-image scores. The research was designed within a psychodynamic framework, more specifically, within the context of object relations theory. A distinction was made between God image and God concept using the definitions provided by Rizzuto. According to Rizzuto (1979), God image is a psychological working internal model that depicts the sort of person that the individual imagines God to be, whereas the God concept is an intellectual and mental-dictionary definition of the word "God."

This article begins by briefly presenting theoretical concepts pertinent to this study and relevant research findings. The remainder of the

---

[Haworth co-indexing entry note]: "The Formation of Adolescents' Image of God: Predictors and Age Gender Differences." Meier, Augustine, and Molisa Meier. Co-published simultaneously in *American Journal of Pastoral Counseling* (The Haworth Pastoral Press, an imprint of The Haworth Press, Inc.) Vol. 7, No. 2, 2004, pp. 91-111; and: *The Image of God and the Psychology of Religion* (ed: Richard Dayringer, and David Oler) The Haworth Pastoral Press, an imprint of The Haworth Press, Inc., 2004, pp. 91-111. Single or multiple copies of this article are available for a fee from The Haworth Document Delivery Service [1-800-HAWORTH, 9:00 a.m. - 5:00 p.m. (EST). E-mail address: docdelivery@haworthpress.com].

http://www.haworthpress.com/web/AJPC
Digital Object Identifier: 10.1300/J062v7n02_07

article presents the research method and results. It concludes with a discussion of the results and the limitations of the study. *[Article copies available for a fee from The Haworth Document Delivery Service: 1-800-HAWORTH. E-mail address: <docdelivery@haworthpress.com> Website: <http://www.HaworthPress.com>* © 2004 by The Haworth Press, Inc. All rights reserved.]

THEORETICAL ASPECTS

Four main theories have been proposed to explain the process by which adolescents develop a personal and unique image of God: religious socialization, self-esteem hypothesis, projection theory, and object relations theory.

Religious Socialization: The focus of the socialization process has been on the "transmission of specific beliefs by parents or organized religion and on the socioeconomic matrix within which beliefs are generated" (Potvin, 1977, p. 44). Views of God are seen as part of a world view which is influenced by education and social status. Parental religious practice has been found to be an important index of the parents' commitment to socialize their children within a particular religious tradition (Carrier, 1965). In a study to assess the relationship of the parental religious socialization process on the development of an image of God, Potvin (1977) observed that parental control discriminated fairly consistently between "those who believe in a loving and a punishing God and those who believe in a loving but non-punishing God" (p. 49). Parental affection failed to produce any significant findings (Potvin, 1977).

Self-Esteem Hypothesis: The self-esteem hypothesis, an extension of the projection hypothesis presented below, assumes that there is an interrelationship between self-esteem and loving God image (Roberts, 1989). It is thought that believers who love themselves will perceive a loving God, while self-rejecting believers will view God as rejecting. Research findings in support of this hypothesis are mixed. A positive relationship has been found to exist between "the extent to which an individual expresses acceptance of self and the extent to which he expresses a belief in an accepting God" (Ellzey, 1961, p. 53). High self-esteem was significantly related to a loving God image (Benson & Spilka, 1973; Chartier & Goehner, 1976; Roberts, 1989; Francis, Gibson & Robbins, 2001). Self-esteem has been observed to positively relate to loving God images and negatively to rejecting or controlling definitions of God (Spilka, Addison & Rosensohn, 1975). However, other studies did not find a positive correlation between self-esteem and a loving image of God (Potvin, 1977).

Projection Theory: Freud (1927) speculated that one's images of God are projections of father images (Potvin, 1977; Roberts, 1989). According to psychoanalytic theory, "the most basic dimension contained in the paternal image is law in as much as the father is the one who comes between the mother and the child causing him to rise above the principles of immediate pleasure and introducing the principle of reality into his life" (Vergote, Tamayo et al., 1969, p. 82).The sources of projection have been expanded by subsequent research. These studies contend that the images of God are projections of mother images (Nelson & Jones, 1957), are influenced by both parents (Vergote, Tamayo et al., 1969), are the images of the preferred parent (Nelson, 1971), the like-sex parent (Spilka et al., 1975), and the self (Benson & Spilka, 1972). Godin and Hallez (1965) and Deconchy (1968) suggest that "conceptions of the male parent are more crucial for females while conceptions of the female parent are more important for males" (Potvin, 1977, p. 44). The evidence in support of projection theory is mixed. Benson and Spilka (1973) found some evidence of like patterning between self- and God-images. However, Spilka, Addison and Rosensohn (1975) found no clear support that subjects in a sample of Catholic youths imagined God as a projection of either themselves or of their parents.

Object Relations Theory: A more recent extension of the projection hypothesis is object relations theory which was introduced to the study of the image of God by Rizzuto (1979). Two major concepts derived from object relations theory applicable to the study of the formation of an image of God are: formation of internal representations and the process of separation and individuation.

Formation of Internal Representations: Object relations theory considers the infant-mother relationship to be the most important of all relationships (Klein, 1975; Fairbairn, 1952; Winnicott, 1960/1965; Mahler, Pine & Bergman, 1975; Bowlby, 1988). In the course of the infant's interactions with the mother (or principal caregiver), the infant has both pleasant and unpleasant experiences. Pleasant experiences originate from the infant having its needs met (e.g., being fed) whereas unpleasant experiences originate from feeling frustrated in not having its needs met. Due to the infant's immature ego and perceptual processes, it experiences the mother which responds positively to the child's needs as being a different person from the one who frustrates the infant. The two sets of experiences, the pleasant and unpleasant, become organized to form two different perceptions of mother. The person who responds to the infant's needs is perceived as being the 'good-mother' whereas the person who frustrates the infant is considered as being the 'bad-mother.'

Parallel to forming representations of the mother, the infant also forms representations of self. When the mother responds positively to the infant's needs, the infant experiences pleasure and feels good about self. However, when the mother fails to respond to the infant's needs, the infant experiences displeasure and feels bad about self. The infant therefore forms two representations of self, the 'good self' and the 'bad self.'

With continued maturation, the images of the mother and self become integrated in the sense that the mother and self are seen as being both good and bad. These internal representations become the working model (Bowlby, 1988) by which the person interprets information and events and interacts with persons. Although a certain level of integration has occurred between the good and bad aspects of other (e.g., mother) and self, the person will retain the propensity to think of others as being either good or bad, loving and punishing, etc. For the child who has developed a positive image of mother, he/she will turn to this positive image in times of stress, disappointments, emotional hurts, etc., to seek comfort and support. That is, the mother becomes the internalized good object to which the child can turn for comfort and soothing.

The Separation-Individuation Process: The infant begins its first months of post-natal life in a state of "oneness" with the mother (Kaplan, 1978). The infant and the mother are fused; they form a symbiotic relationship (Mahler et al., 1975). Within one or two months after birth, the infant begins the dual process of separating from the mother and striving towards its own individuality (Mahler et al., 1975). Separating and individuating are two distinct but parallel processes. One of the first behavioral manifestations of separating from the mother is the infant/child turning from a lap-baby to one who begins to crawl, and then walk. Parallel to this process, the infant begins to individuate, to become his/her own person. A clear manifestation of this is the child's assertion of "no." Separating and individuating bring with them their particular conflicts and anxieties. In separating from his/her mother the child discovers the world and develops a love-affair with it. The child is torn between pursuing his/her pursuit of individuality and maintaining the bond with the mother. To pursue one's individuality, one risks losing emotional connection with mother and being alone and experiencing loneliness. On the other hand, by rigorously maintaining the emotional connection with mother, one risks psychologically losing oneself. The major task at this age is to achieve a balance between being one's own person and at the same time maintaining an emotional bond with the mother. The separation-individuation process is worked through for the first time when the child is between two and four years of age. It is reworked each time that the person meets a transition in life such as going through adolescence, leaving home, children leaving home, etc. Each time that this dual process is worked through, that is, each time that the person leaves the good-object (e.g., mother) in pursuit of individuality, the person will experience being alone and empty; he/she will miss the presence of the significant other (e.g., mother, children).

According to object relations theory, the person's childhood relationships with significant others form the basis for all relationships including that with God. With regard to the formation of an image of God, the positive and negative attributes of these early relationships are used as analogies to portray what God might be like.

Rizzuto (1974, 1976, 1979, 1982), on the basis of her extensive case studies, suggested that one's image of God develops within the matrix of the mother-child relationship. She added that God representation continues to develop with a variety of significant others contributing to the person's ever growing and expanding image of God. McDargh (1983, 1986) suggests that a child's images of God have their origin in the relationship with the other. The quality and nature of the child's inner representational world, derived from his/her experiences in relating with significant others, affects the image of God that he or she develops.

This research is guided by object relations theory and hypothesizes that a person's image of the mother, father, etc., contributes in a unique way to the formation of the person's image of God. The image of God, therefore, is a composite of the representations of significant others and of self.

RESEARCH FINDINGS

Age and Gender Differences

Vergote, Tamayo and associates (1969) observed that the image of God became more maternal as a person moved from high school to college status. They state that for high school students the image of God was definitely closer to the father than to the mother (in corresponding qualities); this was not the case for college students where there was no significant difference. Vergote, Tamayo and associates (1969) also observed that with increasing age there is an increase in maternal characteristics in the parental images among American males but not among the females and that the image of God comprises both maternal and paternal characteristics. However, their data showed that the paternal characteristics were more accentuated than the maternal ones, thus the "image of God is closer to the image of father when all characteristics are considered, as well as when just maternal or just paternal characteristics are considered" (p. 86).

Dickie et al. (1997) found that when parents were perceived as nurturing and powerful (particularly when mother was perceived as powerful and father as nurturing), children perceived God as both nurturing and powerful. God was perceived more like the father in early childhood and more like the mother or both parents in middle childhood.

Two- or Three-Dimensional God

In his review of the research literature, Roberts (1989) was struck by the fact that subjects, regardless of population and instruments used, "describe God along two distinct . . . dimensions, namely nurturance and discipline" (p. 376). These dimensions have been named differently including: masculine and feminine (Vergote et al., 1969, 1981); traditional Christian (benevolent) and wrathful (Gorsuch, 1968); loving and punishing (Potvin, 1977); loving and controlling (Spilka et al., 1975); and healer and king (Nelson et al., 1985).

Krejci (1998), however, proposed a three-dimensional God. In his study of the relationship of gender to God schemas he observed that the subjects organized their God image around three dimensions: nurturing-judging, controlling-saving, and concrete-abstract. The one and only gender difference was that males placed greater salience on the controlling image. Gerkin (1994), also, hypothesized three images of God based on object relations theory. The three images are: (a) God as the fulfiller of all wishes, (b) God as one who rejects persons, making them feel guilt or shame, and (c) God who is ideal, perfect, leaving humans with a sense of mystery but also haunted, at times, by God's absence.

RESEARCH QUESTIONS

The research questions were formulated with reference to Object Relations Theory and to the research findings.

Given that the objective of this study was to investigate gender and age differences on the formation of images of God and to study the contribution of factors to the formation of adolescents' images of God, the following questions were asked:

1. Are there age differences on the image of God as measured by the Image of God Scale?
2. Are there gender differences on the image of God as measured by the Image of God Scale?
3. Do the adolescents' scores on the maternal and paternal characteristics of their mother and father predict their Image of God as measured by the Image of God Scale?

RESEARCH DESIGN

Research Participants

The sample for this study comprised a combined eighty 12-13 and 16-17 English-speaking male and female students taken from one high school in the Ottawa Carleton Separate School Board, Ottawa, Ontario. The distribution of the sample according to age and gender is summarized in Table 1. The means and standard deviations for the same groups are also provided. The groups did not differ significantly from each other on age and gender.

Research Measures

The instruments designed by Vergote et al. (1969) and Lawrence (1997) were selected for the research because they are flexible and can be used with different populations and for a broad range of questions. As well, they provide numerical data for statistical analysis. In addition to these instruments, a Demographic Information Form was designed to gather demographic data concerning each participant.

Demographic Information Form: This Form contained questions to gather information on age, gender, grade, and primary female and pri-

TABLE 1. The Distribution of the Sample According to Age and Gender with Their Means and Standard Deviations

Age and Gender Group	N	Mean	S.D.
12-13: Males	22	12.64	.66
12-13: Females	19	12.79	.42
16-17: Males	21	16.33	.58
16-17: Females	18	16.22	.55

mary male caregiver. Questions regarding the composition of the family (e.g., intact, single parent), culture of origin, and birth country were not included as these were deemed too sensitive by the Research and Ethic Committees. Based on the information provided regarding the primary caregivers, it is evident that all participants came from intact families, that is, they lived with their birth fathers and mothers.

Richard Lawrence's God-Image Inventory: In determining the dimensions of this inventory, Lawrence (1997, p. 215) was guided by object relations theory. He assumed that one finds the same critical areas of relationship between the God image and the self image. The critical areas of the self-image are feelings of belonging, fundamental goodness, and control. The three topics, belonging, goodness, and control each yield two measurable dimensions of the God image. Lawrence (1997, p. 215) states that the first dimension of each pair is the most primitive and more focused on the self, the second dimension, growing out of the first, is more focused on the object of the relationship. The six dimensions (scales) of the God image emerging from this are: Presence, Challenge, Acceptance, Benevolence, Influence, and Providence. Two more dimensions (scales) were added, namely, Faith and Salience to produce an 8-scale Inventory.

The eight dimensions were operationalized to form an 8-scale, 156 item psychometric questionnaire designed to measure the image of God (Lawrence, 1997). All of the items are scored on a 4-point Likert scale with 1 = Strongly Disagree and 4 = Strongly Agree. The instrument, called the God Image Inventory, produces separate scores for each of the eight scales.

The God-Image Inventory was standardized using 1580 adults. Marital status was not found to correlate with any of its scales. Age, education and gender correlated with the scales. Lawrence reports that the instrument has good reliability and validity (Lawrence, 1997). The eight scales are from moderately to highly inter-correlated.

Lawrence recommends an abbreviated version–3-scale, 36 item–of the God-Image Inventory for the purpose of research. This abbreviated version is called the God-Image Scales (Lawrence, 1997). The three scales recommended and used are:

Presence: This is summed up in "Is God there for me?" In object relations terminology, this captures the impact on the God image of the first belonging question "Do I belong?" In the eyes of the infant this question reads, "Is mother there for me?" (Lawrence, 1997, p. 215).

Challenge: This is summed up in the question "Does God want me to grow?" That is, does God's presence in my life demand that "I move out into and interact with the world around me?" (Lawrence, 1997, p. 216). In human terms, this parallels the emergence of the infant as an individual distinct from its mother.

Acceptance: This scale measures one's goodness. The question asked is "Am I good enough for God to love?" (Lawrence, 1997, p. 216). In human terms, the question asked is "Am I good enough for mother to love?"

For this research, individual scores for the three scales–Presence, Challenge, and Acceptance–were calculated. Since the three scales were highly intercorrelated (Presence + Challenge = .63; Presence + Acceptance = .53; Challenge + Acceptance = .71) and there were no age × gender interactions (see Table 3) a Total God Image Score was calculated by adding the scores for the three scales.

Vergote Questionnaire: Vergote et al. (1969) developed an instrument to derive maternal and paternal images regarding parents and God. The instrument comprises 18 maternal and 18 paternal characteristics which are responded to on a 7-point Likert scale. An example of a maternal characteristic is "who welcomes me with open arms" and an example of paternal characteristic is "protection against danger." This method of gathering data is supported by good validity and reliability data (Vergote et al., 1969, p. 81).

For this research, a scale which contains the 36 characteristics was developed to assess, separately, the subject's image of his/her primary female caregiver and primary male caregiver as the subject experienced them when he/she **was a child**. The same procedure was repeated to assess how the subject experienced his/her primary female caregiver and primary male caregiver **today**. Each item was responded to on a 7-point Likert Scale.

The instrument produces separate scores for the Maternal Characteristics and for the Paternal Characteristics with a maximum score of 126 for each set of characteristics but it does not provide a method to obtain a total score for each participant. To combine the scores for the two sets of characteristics would not be meaningful for this research since the goal of this study is to assess the contribution of Maternal and Paternal Characteristics to the development of the image of God. For example, a combined score of 100 might mean that one person obtained 60 for Maternal Characteristics and 40 for the Paternal Characteristics. For a second person a score of 100 might mean the reverse. Thus, combining the scores for the Maternal and Paternal Characteristics does not provide meaningful data. The researchers therefore computed a total score in terms of a ratio by dividing the Maternal Characteristic by the Paternalistic Score. The ratio gave information regarding the extent to which the Maternal and Paternal Characteristics were integrated. For example, a score of 1.25 indicates a greater presence of Maternal Characteristics than Paternal Characteristics whereas a score of .75 indicates the opposite.

Using the gender of the parent, the two characteristics (Maternal, Paternal, Maternal/Paternal Ratio), and the time frame for which assessment was made (As a Child, Today), this instrument, produced a total of 10 subscales with scores for each. A description of the ten subscales with their acronyms are:

MMoC - The maternal qualities (M) of mother (Mo) experienced as a child (C)
PMoC - The paternal qualities (P) of mother experienced as a child
MFaC - The maternal qualities of father (Fa) experienced as a child
PFaC   - The paternal qualities of father experienced as a child
MMoT - The maternal qualities of mother as experienced today (T)
PMoT - The paternal qualities of mother as experienced today
MFaT - The maternal qualities of father as experienced today
PFaT   - The paternal qualities of father as experienced today
RMoC - The maternal/paternal ratio (R) experienced as a child
RFaC   - The maternal/paternal ratio for father experienced as a child
RMoT - The maternal/paternal ratio for mother as experienced today
RFaT - The maternal/paternal ratio for father as experienced today

The scores for the maternal and paternal characteristics of the Female Caregiver and Male Caregiver as perceived *As a Child* and *Today* were assessed for their ability to predict the participants Total God Image Score as Measured by the Image of God-Scales.

RESEARCH METHOD

Recruitment of Participants

A research proposal was submitted to the Ottawa Carleton Separate School Board requesting authorization to recruit high school students from its schools. After approval by the Board's Research Committee, principals of school were informed of the study. One school expressed interest in the study, provided the name of a contact-teacher and contacted the researcher. The required information sheets, consent forms and testing material were sent to the contact-teacher at the school.

A total number of 112 students participated in the study. Excluded from the study were: (a) those who came from broken and single-parent homes (9 in total) since it is not known how being brought up in a broken home, a single-parent home, etc., affects the formation of a child's image of God, (b) the participants who did not complete the entire set of questionnaires (19 in all), and (c) the fourteen to fifteen year olds (12) in order to maximize the possibility for finding age differences. Thus a total of 80 students or 66 percent of the original pool participated in this study.

Information and Consent Forms

An information sheet describing the nature of the research, emotional risk in taking the research, the right to withdraw from the study, etc., was prepared for the parents. The home-room teacher gave this form to the student to take home for his or her parents. Those who accepted to take part in the study signed a consent form and returned it to the researchers. The participant signed the consent form as well.

Administration and Scoring of the Research Measures

The contact-teacher from the school coordinated the administration of the research material. The researchers met with the contact-teacher to review the procedures regarding confidentiality, obtaining written consent and the administration of the research instruments. The contact-teacher then contacted classroom teachers (home-room teachers) to inform them of the research and to provide those who wished to participate with the required research material. The home-room teacher administered the Demographical Form and the research instruments in a classroom setting. It took approximately 30-45 minutes to complete the battery of questionnaires. All of the material was hand scored by the researchers.

RESULTS

Age and Gender Differences

The first two research questions are: (a) Are there age differences on the image of God as measured by the Image of God Scale and (b) Are there gender differences on the image of God as measured by the Image of God Scale? To investigate these two research questions, the means and standard deviations for the scales, Presence, Acceptance, Challenge and Total God Image Score were calculated. These are presented in Table 2. Using the SPSS 11.0 for Windows Student Version (SPSS Inc., 2001; George & Mallery, 2003), a Multivariate Analysis of Variance (MANOVA) were applied to the data. The results of this analysis are presented in Table 3. The MANOVA produced only one significant finding and that was for age differences on Presence. The means for the 12-13 and 16-17 year age groups and on Presence were 36.85 and 30.97, respectively, and the standard deviations were 7.70 and 9.70, respectively. Thus the 16-17 year age group when compared to the 12-13 year age group scored significantly lower ($F = 9.33$, p. $= 0.00$) on Presence.

Analysis of Predictors

Four multiple regression analyses were performed on Total God Image Scores as measured by the God Image Scales. Blocks of predictors were entered separately according to the time frame from which images were assessed (As a Child, Today) and according to the characteristics assessed (Maternal, Paternal, Maternal/Paternal Ratio). Means and Standard Deviations for Characteristics Derived from the Vergote Questionnaire appear in Table 4.

Prior to and after the regression analyses were performed, the data were checked for violations regarding ratio of cases to independent variables (IV), absence of outliers for IV and the dependent variables (DV), absence of multicollinearity and singularity, normality, linearity,

TABLE 2. Means and Standard Deviations for the Subscales of the Image of God Inventory By Age and Gender

Variable	Presence		Acceptance		Challenge		Total	
	M	SD	M	SD	M	SD	M	SD
Age: 12-13	36.85	7.70	40.73	5.98	38.02	4.84	115.10	17.12
Males	36.12	7.75	39.41	5.68	36.91	4.80	111.50	18.70
Females	37.68	7.76	42.26	6.10	39.31	4.70	119.26	14.50
Age: 16-17	30.97	9.70	38.23	8.55	38.02	4.84	106.48	23.01
Males	32.00	8.66	39.38	7.37	36.71	7.28	108.47	19.29
Females	29.77	10.91	36.89	9.80	37.39	8.68	104.17	27.12
Males	34.12	8.37	39.40	6.48	38.81	6.06	110.02	18.82
Females	33.84	10.12	39.65	8.44	38.38	6.89	111.92	22.61
Population	33.98	9.16	39.51	7.40	37.53	6.47	110.90	20.54

TABLE 3. Summary of Multivariate Analysis of Variance: Relationship of Age and Gender with Scores on Acceptance, Challenge and Presence (N = 80)

Variable	Source	d.f.	MS	F	p.
Acceptance	Age	1	145.02	2.71	.10
	Error	76	53.47		
Challenge	Age	1	22.37	.53	.47
	Error	76	42.38		
Presence	Age	1	720.60	9.33	.00
	Error	76	77.26		
Acceptance	Gender	1	1.28	.02	.88
	Error	76	53.47		
Challenge	Gender	1	48.67	1.17	.28
	Error	76	42.38		
Presence	Gender	1	1.54	.01	.89
	Error	76	77.26		
Acceptance	Gender × Age	1	142.01	2.66	.11
	Error	76	53.47		
Challenge	Gender × Age	1	14.91	.35	.56
	Error	76	42.38		
Presence	Gender × Age	1	70.62	.91	.34
	Error	76	77.26		

and homoscedascity of residuals (Tabachnick & Fidell, 2001, pp. 117-121; Norusis, 1993). No violations were observed; therefore the analysis of the data continued.

The alphas obtained in the analysis of variance (ANOVA) for the regression lines, were adjusted using the Bonferroni test statistic

TABLE 4. Means and Standard Deviations for Scales Derived from the Vergote Questionnaire (N = 80)

Variable	Mean	S.D.
MMoC	108.26	14.10
PMoC	95.55	18.96
MFaC	95.01	21.12
PFaC	106.46	15.85
MMoT	105.37	20.38
PMoT	95.57	20.75
MFaT	91.91	26.94
PFaT	101.75	19.62
RMoC	1.18	.28
RFaC	.90	.20
RMoT	1.14	.26
RFaT	.91	.22

M = maternal qualities; P = paternal qualities; MO = mother; Fa = father; C = from the perspective of a Child; T = from the perspective of today; R = the maternal/paternal ratio

(Pedhazur, 1997, p. 385). This involves dividing the alpha level (e.g., 0.05) by the number of tests performed.

In the first multiple regression analysis, the data were analyzed using as regressors MMoC, PMoC, MFaC, and PFaC. The dependent variable was the Total God Image Score. The results from this analysis are summarized in Table 5. The regression was a fair fit (R^2_{adj} = 21%) and the overall relationship was significant ($F_{4, 75}$ = 6.11, p. < 0.00). With other variables held constant, Total God Image Scores were negatively related to PMoC and PFaC. Only the effect for MMoC was significant (t_{75} = 3.69, p < 0.00). This means that the participants' assessment of the maternal characteristics of their mothers seen from the perspective of a child is a fair predictor of their current image of God (Total God Image Score).

In the second multiple regression analysis, the data were analyzed using as regressors MMoT, PMoT, MFaT and PFaT and as the dependent variable the Total God Image Score. Table 6 summarizes the results from this analysis. The regression was a rather poor fit (R^2_{adj} =18%) but the overall relationship was significant ($F_{4, 74}$ = 5.28, p. < 0.00). Total God Image Scores, with other variables held constant, were negatively related to PMoT and PFaT. Only the effect for MMoT was significant (t_{75} = 3.22, p < 0.00). Despite it being significant, MMoT is not a good predictor of a participant's current image of God as determined by the Total God Image Scores.

TABLE 5. Standard Multiple Regression of Maternal and Paternal Characteristics from Child's Perspective on the Formation of Image of God

Variable	God Image DV	MMoC	PMoC	MFaC	PFaC	B	β
MMoC	.45					.68	.47
PMoC	.29	.49				−.27	−.07
MFaC	.30	.48	.63			.18	.19
PFaC	.02	.35	−.05	.33		−7.36	−2.10
Means	110.90	108.26	95.55	95.01	106.46	Intercept = 55.36	R = .50 R² = .25 Adj R² = .21
S.D.	20.54	14.10	18.96	21.12	15.85		

$F_{4,75} = 6.11$, p. < 0.00 (Bonferroni adjusted F = 0.01); $t_{1,75} = 3.69$, p < 0.00

TABLE 6. Standard Multiple Regression of Maternal and Paternal Characteristics from Today's Perspective on the Formation of Image of God

Variable	God Image DV	MMoT	PMoT	MFaT	PFaT	B	β
MMoT	.45					.49	.49
PMoT	.23	.63				−.13	.14
MFaT	.32	.62	.23			.13	.12
PFaT	.12	.42	.02	.00		−.16	−.16
Means	110.70	105.37	95.57	92.29	101.91	Intercept = 75.72	R = .47 R² = .22 Adj R² = .18
S.D.	20.59	20.38	20.75	26.90	19.69		

$F_{4,74} = 5.28$, p < 0.00 (Bonferroni adjusted F = 0.01); t $_{1,75} = 3.22$, p < 0.00

In the following two multiple regression analyses, the regressors comprised the ratios obtained by dividing the maternal scores by the paternal scores. The purpose was to examine the relationship of participants' scores which combined both the maternal and paternal characteristics of their mothers and their fathers, respectively, to the Total God Image Score.

In the third multiple regression analysis, the regressors were RMoC and RFaC. The regression was a poor fit ($R^2_{adj} = 5\%$) and the overall relationship between the regressors and the Total God Image Scores was not significant ($F_{2, 77} = 3.00$, p. $= 0.056$). This means that the ratio of paternal to maternal scores (characteristics) is not a good predictor of a participant's current image of God.

In the fourth multiple regression analysis, the regressors were RMoT and RFaT. The regression was a very poor fit ($R^2_{adj} = 6\%$) but the overall relationship was significant ($F_{2, 76} = 3.56$, p. $= 0.03$). Total God Image Scores, with other variables held constant, were positively related to RMoT and RFaT. Only the effect of FRaT was significant ($t_{75} = 2.63$, $p < 0.01$). Despite the overall significant relationship, the FRaT is not a good predictor of a participant's current image of God as measured by the Total God Image Score. These data are summarized in Table 7.

In summary, only MMoC is a fair predictor of participants' image of God as determined by the Total God Image Score. That is, the participants' assessments of the maternal characteristics of their mothers are a fair predictor of their image of God.

DISCUSSION

Age and Gender Differences: This study produced no gender differences and no age $\times$ gender interaction on the three scales derived from the God Image Scales (Presence, Acceptance, Challenge) and only one age difference on the Scale, Presence (see Table 8). This finding, in object relations terminology, means that the 16-17 year age group does not have as strong a sense of God's presence as the 12-13 year age group.

TABLE 7. Standard Multiple Regression of Maternal/Parental Characteristic Ratio from Today's Perspective on the Formation of Image of God

Variable	God Image DV	RMoT	RFaT	B	β
RMoT	.05			8.89	.11
RFaT	.27	−.20		27.16	.29
Means	110.69	1.14	.91	Intercept = 75.92	R = .29 R² = .09 Adj R² = .06
S.D.	20.59	.26	.22		

$F_{2,76} = 3.56$, $p < 0.03$ (Bonferroni adjusted F = 0.03); $t_{1,75} = 2.63$, $p = 0.01$

TABLE 8. God Scale: Correlations and Probabilities

	Acceptance	Challenge	Presence	ExpGod
Acceptance	1.00	.69 p = .000	.50 p = .000	.85 p = .00
Challenge		1.00	.56 p = .000	.84 p = .00
Presence			1.00	.83 p = .00
ExpGod				1.00

Developmentally, it appears that the 12-13 year age group's image of God is a continuation of how they experienced God in the previous years. There has been no rupture in how they experience God. However, when the same adolescents reach the age of 16-17, they are in the process of defining themselves and refining their image of God. Late adolescence, therefore, is a time to rework their earlier images. As they rework their earlier images, they distance themselves from the earlier images, find themselves in a transition state (in between state) and acquire a revised image of God. From an object relations theory perspective, they are experiencing their second major separation from significant others. This entails letting go of connections and asserting one's independence and autonomy. This leads to the feeling of being alone and being without the presence of the other. This shift between the two age groups is consistent with a much earlier finding where the 17-19-year age group scored significantly lower than other age groups including a 12-13 age group on finding meaningful things around which to organize their lives (Meier, 1974, p. 385).

Lawrence (1997) standardized the Image of God Inventory on 1580 adults. Adolescents were not included in the sample. He reported that age showed some correlations with the subscales. However, he did not report the age distribution of his sample and therefore one cannot compare the results from the two studies. It appears important to include younger age groups when doing research on God image because of the developmental factor referred to above. For example, Vergote and associates (1969) observed differences in the image of God between high school students and college students. It is important to ascertain whether the observed changes are related to the lower late adolescents' score or to the higher college students' scores. In other words, how do the college students differ from 12-13 year old teenagers, for example?

To assess for age differences, it is necessary to include a wide range of age groups.

Predictors of God Image Score: Research is not clear as to whether the image of God is a projection of the image of father (Freud, 1927), mother (Nelson & Jones, 1957), like-sex parent (Spilka et al., 1975), the preferred parent (Nelson, 1971), or both parents (Vergote et al., 1969). Research has been inconclusive in finding significant relationships between the projections of persons and the image of God. This might in part be related to instruments used and age groups studied. In this study, the participants' experience of their mother in terms of her maternal characteristics (as seen when a child) was found to be a fair predictor of their image of God scores. A participants' current experience of the mother in terms of maternal characteristics is a weak predictor but is consistent with the idea that the maternal characteristics of the mother are projected onto a person's image of God. This finding is also consistent with object relations theory which states that the images that a person forms of childhood caregivers, such as mother and father, are prototypes for future relationships, that is, they are working models in the way others, including God, are perceived and related to.

Limitations: One of the limitations is the small sample size which did not allow multiple regression analysis according to age, gender and age × gender interactions. In this research, the effect of regressors on God image scores were not investigated for age and gender differences. This indeed is a weakness of the study. A larger sample is required to conduct a more refined analysis of the effect of regressors on the dependent variable.

A second limitation is that there are few adequate instruments available to do more refined research on the image of God. The God Image Inventory (Lawrence, 1997), for example, is useful to measure age and gender differences for adults on eight scales. However, it is not designed to assess the influence of maternal and paternal characteristics which apparently depict a two-dimension God image (Vergote et al., 1969, 1981; Gorsuch, 1968; Potvin, 1977; Spilka et al., 1975; Nelson et al., 1985). Although Vergote et al.'s scale (1969) provides measures to assess for maternal and paternal characteristics, it does not indicate how the two scales can be combined to assess the differential between maternal and paternal characteristics in significant others and God. The technique which provides a ratio by dividing the score for maternal characteristics by the score for paternal characteristics did not seem adequate. Therefore, to test the significant contribution of parents, significant other, etc., in the child's development of an image of God, more refined instruments are required. Perhaps a factor analysis could be applied to the items that constitute the maternal and paternal characteristics to determine whether there indeed are two factors.

A third limitation is the nature of the sample which came from one Roman Catholic School. All of the participants were from intact families, that is, they were living with their birth fathers and mothers. It is necessary to assess the impact of one's culture and of one's religious or spiritual orientation on one's image of God. An interesting research topic would be the study of the impact of divorce, single parents, and same-gender parents on a child's image of God.

Fourth, one part of this study used a retrospective approach to garner the participants' images of their parents in terms of maternal and paternal characteristics as they experienced them to be when the participant was a child. As with all retrospective studies, the participants' image of their parents might indeed be distorted and colored by their current experience of their parents.

Despite these limitations, the study does open the way for further research in this area. It suggests that one's early images of significant others influences one's image of God. To carry out research from an object relations perspective, new instruments are required which have the capacity to measure the differential influence from many significant persons on the formation of a composite image of God.

REFERENCES

Benson, P., & Spilka, B. (1973). God image as a function of self-esteem and locus of control. *Journal for the Scientific Study of Religion, 12*, 297-310.

Bowlby, J. (1988). *A secure base: Parent-child attachment and healthy human development.* New York: Basic Books.

Brokaw, B.F., & Edwards, K.J. (1994). The relationship of the God image to level of object relations development. *Journal of Psychology and Theology, 22*, 352-371.

Carrier, H. (1965). *The sociology of religious belonging.* New York: Herder & Herder.

Chartier, M.R. & Goehner, L.A. (1976). A study of the relationship of parent-adolesecent communication, self-esteem, and God image. *Journal of Psychology and Religion, 4*(Summer), 227-232.

Deconchy, J. (1968). God and parent images. In A. Godin (Ed.), *From cry to word.* Brussles, Bel.: Lumen Vitae, 85-94.

Dickie, J.R., Eshleman, A.K., Merasco, D.M., Shepard, A., Vander Wilt, M., & Johnson, M. (1997). Parent-child relationships and children's images of God. *Journal for the Scientific Study of Religion, 36*, 25-43.

Ellzey, C.H. (1961). *Relationships among acceptance of self, acceptance of others, and belief in an accepting God.* Unpublished doctoral dissertation, Columbia University (University Microfilms No. 61-1074).

Fairbairn, W.R.D. (1952). *An object-relations theory of personality.* New York: Basic Books.

Francis, L.J., Gibson, H.M., & Robbins, M. (2001). God images and self-worth among adolescents in Scotland. *Mental Health, Religion and Culture, 4*(2), 103-108.

Freud, S. (1927). *Totem and taboo.* New York: Republic.

George, D., & Mallery, P. (2003). *SPSS for Windows step by step: A simple guide and reference, 11.0 update.* Toronto: Pearson Education, pp. 177-206.

Gerkin, C. (1994). Projective identification and the image of God: Reflections on object relations theory and the psychology of religion. In B.H. Childs & D.V. Waanders (Eds.), *The treasure of earthen vessels: Explorations in theological anthropology in honor of James N. Lapsley,* Louisville, KY: Westminster John Knox Press, 52-65.

Godin, A., & Hallez, M. (1965). Parental Images and divine paternity. In A. Godin (Ed.), *From religious experience to a religious attitude,* Chicago: Loyola University Press, 65-96.

Gorsuch, R.L. (1968). The conceptualization of God as seen in adjective ratings. *Journal for the Scientific Study of Religion, 7,* 56-64.

Kaplan, L. (1976). *Oneness and separateness.* New York: Simon & Schuster.

Klein, M. (1975). *Love, guilt and reparation and other works 1921-1945.* London: Hogarth Press. (Volume 3).

Krejci, M.J. (1998). A gender comparison of God schemas: A multidimensional scaling analysis. *International Journal for the Psychology of Religion, 8*(1), 57-66.

Lawrence, R.T. (1997). Measuring the image of God: The God image inventory and the God image scales. *Journal of Psychology and Theology, 28*(2), 214-226.

Mahler, M., Pine, F., & Bergman, A. (1975). *The psychological birth of the human infant.* New York: Basic Books.

McDargh, J. (1983). *Psychoanalytic object relations theory and the study of religion: On faith and the imagining of God.* New York: University Press of America.

McDargh, J. (1986). God, mother and me: An object relational perspective on religious material. *Pastoral Psychology, 34,* 251-263.

Meier, A. (1974). Purpose-in-Life Test: Age and Sex Differences. *Journal of Clinical Psychology, 30*(3), 384-386.

Nelson, H.M., Cheek, N.H., & Au., P. (1985). Gender differences in images of God. *Journal for the Scientific Study of Religion, 24,* 396-402.

Nelson, M.O. (1971). The concept of God and feelings toward parents. *Journal of Individual Psychology, 27,* 46-49.

Nelson, M.O., & Jones, E.M. (1957). An application of the Q-technique to the study of religious concepts. *Psychological Reports, 3,* 293-297.

Norusis, M. (1993). *SPSS for Windows; base system user's guide, release 6.0.* Chicago: SPSS Inc., pp. 311-365.

Pedhazur, E.J. (1997). *Multiple regression in behavioral research: Explanation and prediction.* Toronto, Harcourt College Publishers.

Potvin, R.H. (1977). Adolescent God images. *Review of Religious Research, 19*(1), 43-53.

Rizzuto, A.M. (1974). Object relations and the formation of the image of God. *British Journal of Medical Psychology, 47,* 83-99.

Rizzuto, A.M. (1976). Freud, God, the devil and the theory of object representation. *International Review of Psycho-Analysis, 3,* 165-180.

Rizzuto, A.M. (1979). *The birth of the living God.* Chicago: The Chicago University Press.

Rizzuto, A.M. (1982). The father and the child's representation of God: A developmental approach. In S.H. Cath, A.R. Gurwitt, & A.M. Ross (Eds.), *Father and child,* Boston: Little, Brown, 357-381.

Roberts, C.W. (1989). Imagining God: Who is created in whose image? *Review of Religious Research, 30*(4), 375-386.

Spilka, B., Addison, J. & Rosensohn, M. (1975). Parents, self and God: A test of competing theories of individual-religion relationships. *Review of Religious Research, 16* (Spring), 154-165.

Spilka, B., & Schmidt, G. (1983). General attribution theory for the psychology of religion: The influence of even-character on attribution to God. *Journal for the Scientific Study of Religion, 22,* 326-339.

SPSS Inc. (2001). *The SPSS 110.0 Windows Student Version.* New Jersey.

Tabachnick, B.G., & Fidell, L.S. (2001). *Using multivariate statistics.* Toronto: Alllyn & Bacon.

Vergote, A., & Tamayo, A. (1981). *The parental figures and the representations of God: A psychological and cross-cultural study.* The Hague: Mouton.

Vergote, A., Tamayo, A., Pasquali, L., Bonami, M., Pattyn, M-R, & Custers, A. (1969). Concept of God and parental images. *Journal for the Scientific Study of Religion, 8*(1), 79-87.

Winnicott, D. (1960/1965). The theory of the parent-infant relationship. In D. Winnicott, *The maturational processes and the facilitating environment.* New York: International Universities Press, pp. 37-55.

Index